JEWS
AND
MONEY

ALSO BY ABRAHAM H. FOXMAN
AND AVAILABLE FROM
PALGRAVE MACMILLAN

The Deadliest Lies:

The Israel Lobby and the Myth of Jewish Control

JEWS AND MONEY

THE STORY OF A STEREOTYPE

ABRAHAM H. FOXMAN

palgrave
macmillan

First published in 2010 by PALGRAVE MACMILLAN® in the United
States—a division of St. Martin's Press LLC, 175 Fifth Avenue, New York,
NY 11010.

Where this book is distributed in the UK, Europe and the rest of the
world, this is by Palgrave Macmillan, a division of Macmillan Publishers
Limited, registered in England, company number 785998, of
Houndmills, Basingstoke, Hampshire RG21 6XS.

Palgrave Macmillan is the global academic imprint of the above
companies and has companies and representatives throughout the
world.

Palgrave® and Macmillan® are registered trademarks in the United
States, the United Kingdom, Europe and other countries.

ISBN: 978-0-230-62385-9

Library of Congress Cataloging-in-Publication Data

Foxman, Abraham H.
    Jews and money : the story of a stereotype / Abe Foxman.
      p.   cm.
    ISBN 978-0-230-62385-9 (hardback)
    1. Antisemitism—United States.   2. Jews—United States.
3. Jewish capitalists and financiers—United States.   4. United States—
Ethnic relations.   I. Title.
DS146.U6F69   2010
305.892'4073—dc22

                                                                    201173

A catalogue record of the book is available from the British Library.

Design by Letra Libre

First edition: November 2010

10   9   8   7   6   5   4   3   2   1

Printed in the United States of America.

CONTENTS

To my wife, Golda, and our children,
Michelle and Ariel, son-in-law, Dan,
And my grandchildren, Leila, Gideon, and Amirit

For their love and encouragement

To all who support ADL's efforts to fight
bigotry, stereotypes, and anti-Semitism.

FOREWORD

ews and Money—a provocative title for a provocative book. Abe Foxman wants your attention!

As Director over many years of the Anti-Defamation League, he has a strong sense of mission, fighting bigotry in all its forms, and most particularly lingering anti-Semitism.

The word "lingering" is mine, not Abe Foxman's. My sense is that the stereotype of the avaricious Jew, isolated and insulated from the broader society, has been substantially reduced over my now long lifetime. That is a genuine achievement of an open and tolerant American society.

But Abe is a concerned man. "Lingering" doesn't mean absence. Stereotypes are hard to kill. The devastating financial crisis—the sense of unfairness, of loss of control, of lost hopes—provides fertile ground for anger, for scapegoating, for renewing ancient prejudices. And when a few highly publicized miscreants—Mr. Madoff is one prime example—can be identified by a particular religious affiliation and practice, the potential for reinforcing a stereotype is real.

Jews and Money is an eloquent plea to understand the danger— to resist that temptation to associate a complicated, agonizing, and hard to understand financial crisis with a specific ethnic group, however unfounded the relationship.

Foxman is forceful and convincing in setting the record straight, reaching back in history to identify the sources of anti-Semitic instincts, the twisting and manipulation of Jewish history and traditions.

In my view, he may underplay the progress that has been made, at least in this country, in ameliorating old social and religious prejudices and shibboleths. Three Jewish members of the Supreme Court, admired leaders of the financial world, prominent politicians, widely influential writers and intellectuals all taken for granted.

But I also realize I am not directly "in the line of fire." Foxman has plenty of evidence from the long history of prejudice to justify his sensitivities and forebodings. The battle for tolerance and understanding is never really over, and never will be in the absence of vigilance.

In his forceful writing, Foxman brings a unique and convincing perspective to that effort. We need to remain on guard to understand and to respond to his concerns. That provocative title will demand attention!

Paul Volcker

Former Chairman, Federal Reserve Board

1

THE
BERNIE MADOFF
MOMENT

On the evening of December 11, 1995, businessman Aaron Feuerstein was with family and friends at a restaurant in Boston, Massachusetts. It was his seventieth birthday, and a group of well-wishers had gathered to throw him a surprise party.

In the midst of the festivities, someone walked in with horrifying news. "It's the factory. A boiler exploded. People are hurt, and the buildings are on fire."

No one had to ask, "What factory?" Everyone understood the man was referring to Malden Mills, the textile plant that Aaron Feuerstein's grandfather had built in 1906 and that Aaron himself had managed for almost thirty years.

Within the hour, Feuerstein and his friends were part of a large crowd of onlookers, watching firefighters battle the blaze. It had grown into a six-alarm conflagration, drawing 200 firefighters from as far away as New Hampshire and Boston.

What happened in the days and weeks that followed has become a classic story of business and personal ethics, one that I'm sure will continue to be told for generations to come. As I'll explain, it's also an important story for what it reveals about our society's attitudes toward Jews and Judaism. This is an aspect of the Aaron Feuerstein saga that few people have noticed or commented on. Yet it's deeply relevant and profoundly important today, with our economic and social turmoil and as age-old prejudices and animosities have once again reared their heads, fomenting resentment and dividing communities.

The 1995 fire at Malden Mills wasn't just bad news for Feuerstein's company—it was a potentially devastating blow to an already depressed post-industrial community.

Malden Mills employed 2,400 people, many of them recent immigrants from countries ranging from Italy, Portugal, and Israel to the Dominican Republic. Thousands of people relied on the textile business for their survival. Now, many of them had rushed to the scene and were watching their dreams of the future literally going up in smoke.

Paul Coorey was the president of Local 311 of the Union of Needletrades, Industrial and Textile Employees, which represented many of the workers at Malden Mills. A few days later, he recalled the scene: "I was standing there seeing the mill burn with my son, who also worked there, and he looked at me and said, 'Dad, we just lost our jobs.' Years of our lives seemed gone."

When the flames finally subsided, three of the four factory buildings had been destroyed. (The fourth had been saved, in part, through the heroic damage-control efforts of a team of employees that battled the blaze even after firefighters declared it hopeless.) Thirty-three employees had been injured, though thankfully none had died. The damage was estimated at some $500 million. Families throughout northeastern Massachusetts were in despair, wondering where their next paycheck was coming from.

Many people in Aaron Feuerstein's position would have broken down under the shock. But Feuerstein refused to shed a tear. He bolstered his spirits by recalling a favorite passage from Shakespeare's *King Lear,* in which the distraught monarch vows not to weep although his heart should "break into a hundred thousand flaws." Feuerstein was marshalling his strength for the biggest challenge of his business career—figuring out a way to save Malden Mills and the families who depended upon it.

In truth, even before the 1995 fire, Malden Mills and Aaron Feuerstein had represented something quite unusual in the textile industry. Founded as a knitting company, Malden Mills had experimented with various kinds of fabrics and manufacturing processes throughout the first half of the twentieth century. In the 1970s, it bet big on what proved to be a passing fad—the fake fur craze. When sales of the synthetic material plummeted in the early 1980s, Malden Mills had to lay off hundreds of workers in order to avoid bankruptcy. Aaron Feuerstein, by now the CEO, was personally devastated and vowed to avoid such a calamity in the future if he possibly could.

The company's salvation appeared in the form of a new material developed by its researchers. Called Polarfleece, it was a unique polyester blend that wicked moisture away from the body while providing exceptional warmth. Polarfleece—later renamed Polartec—became a favorite fabric among hikers, campers, and winter sports lovers. Companies like Patagonia, L.L. Bean, and Lands' End sold thousands of garments made from Polartec manufactured by Malden Mills. Polartec was also an early example of environmentally friendly manufacturing: Made largely from recycled polyester fabric and even plastic soda bottles, it provided an economically valuable application for materials that would otherwise be piling up in landfills or polluting waterways. The popularity of Polartec gave Malden Mills a new lease on life.

Most remarkable, throughout the bust-and-boom years of the sixties, seventies, and eighties, Aaron Feuerstein and Malden Mills remained committed to Lawrence, Massachusetts. During these years, hundreds of textile companies were shutting down plants in the Northeast and moving to locations in the South or in the poorer countries of the developing world—Haiti, Venezuela, Bangladesh, Malaysia, Kenya. In the process, they saved countless millions in employee salaries and benefits, enriching their bottom lines and their shareholders.

But Feuerstein resisted this trend. Not only did Malden Mills remain in Lawrence, it continued to negotiate fair contracts with its unionized workforce. One union official described Feuerstein this way: "He believes in the process of collective bargaining and he believes that if you pay people a fair amount of money, and give them good benefits to take care of their families, they will produce for you." By the time of the 1995 fire, Malden Mills workers were earning some of the highest wages in the textile business, averaging around $12.50 per hour.

Under the circumstances, many observers assumed that the blaze would become an opportunity for Aaron Feuerstein to do what most business people would have done years earlier. He could take the money from his insurance policy on the mill (around $300 million) and use it to relocate the company to some more "business-friendly" location. As for the people of Lawrence—well, they'd have to fend for themselves. Few people would have faulted Feuerstein for choosing this path. After all, that's the way business works, isn't it?

But they didn't know Aaron Feuerstein.

His response to the fire began two days later, when paychecks were due to his workers. No one would have been shocked if the checks had been late. But Feuerstein ordered not only that every check be delivered in full and on time, but that a planned Christmas bonus of $275 be included in each envelope. (He also added a note for each worker: "Do not despair. God bless each of you.")

Then, on the evening of December 14, Feuerstein rose to address over a thousand Malden Mills employees who had gathered in the gym of Central Catholic High School to learn what their future would be. "I will get right to my announcement," he said. "For the next 30 days—and it might be more—all our employees will be paid their full salaries. But over and above the money, the most important thing Malden Mills can do for our workers is to get you back to work. By January 2, we will restart operations, and within ninety days we will be fully operational."

The news stunned the crowd. After a moment of shocked silence, they broke into cheers.

Later that same night, Feuerstein made the rounds of Lawrence's leading charitable organizations, delivering donations as he did every holiday season. In all, he disbursed $80,000 in gifts to groups like the Salvation Army and the local soup kitchen.

Feuerstein kept his word to the workers. He ended up paying full wages to his idled employees for up to four months while the plant was rebuilt and new machinery was purchased and installed. The total cost of those salaries was around $25 million. In addition to the $300 million insurance settlement, Malden Mills invested another $100 million in rebuilding the plant, creating a state-of-the-art textile factory that was the first to be built in New England in more than a century. By February, more than 70 percent of the workers were back at their jobs. Within two years, the plant was producing more Polartec than ever.

It would be wonderful to close the story of Aaron Feuerstein and his remarkable company right here. Unfortunately, life doesn't always provide a fairy-tale ending.

The enormous debt that Feuerstein assumed in order to finance the rebuilding of the Lawrence factory eventually caught up with the company. After a business slump in 2001, Malden Mills was forced into Chapter 11 bankruptcy. The company went through several re-organizations during the next eight years, eventually emerging under a new name (Polartec, LLC) and a modernized business model. Feuerstein—by now in his late seventies—lost control of the business in 2004 and was forced to step down by the creditors who held majority shares. The magnificent family business tradition his grandfather had established and that Aaron Feuerstein had brought to fruition was no more.

In some quarters—not many—the financial troubles of Malden Mills were a cause for rejoicing. One cynical economic commentator used the bankruptcy as an opportunity to mock Feuerstein in a Christmas Eve column titled, "Altruism? Bah, Humbug." The writer's central idea was that Aaron Feuerstein's generosity to the workers was the *cause* of the company's collapse, and that if the CEO had been more ruthless in his behavior, the firm might have sur-vived without having to resort to bankruptcy.

I suppose this is possible. But the economic troubles of Malden Mills didn't begin with the 1995 fire. The truth is, it's amazing that Aaron Feuerstein managed to keep a textile company operating in Massachusetts, employing thousands of local workers, and compet-ing successfully with low-cost producers from lower-cost states and countries around the world. The company's years of survival through the twentieth century and into the twenty-first strike me as a testament to Feuerstein's business acumen, not the reverse.

Even today, Polartec is defying the odds. Polartec fabric continues to be produced in Lawrence, Massachusetts, though the factory operates on a more limited scale, employing between 835 and 1,000 workers at a time depending on seasonal demand. Who is to say those jobs are valueless? Surely not the thousands of working-class people whose mortgage and tuition payments and grocery bills have been covered by Polartec paychecks for all these years. Humbug? No—good business and humane behavior rolled into one.

In the years since 1995, many people have come to know part of the story of Aaron Feuerstein and Malden Mills. President Bill Clinton honored Feuerstein during his 1996 State of the Union address, and the CBS news magazine *Sixty Minutes* ran a feature about him in 2003, dubbing him "The Mensch of Malden Mills." (*Mensch* is a Yiddish word that describes a person of honor and integrity.) Feuerstein has become something of a folk hero and a role model for thousands of people, especially in business.

But not everyone who admires Aaron Feuerstein knows about the source of his powerful personal morality. Feuerstein happens to be an Orthodox Jew, who draws his guidance on all ethical matters from Jewish tradition, religious teachings, and ultimately the Hebrew scriptures. And this aspect of Feuerstein's story—so central to his life, yet largely neglected in the mainstream accounts—is the one I want to emphasize here.

As many news stories about Feuerstein noted, he is a lover of great literature who enjoys memorizing poetry by Shakespeare and Emily Dickinson. But far more important to him is the Torah, which he makes a point of reading every night.

In applying biblical teachings to practical business questions, Feuerstein is following a family tradition. In a speech on "The People and the Community" at MIT, he recalled his grandfather's practice of distributing paychecks to the workers at Malden Mills before sunset, citing the book of Deuteronomy (24:14–15) as justification: "Do not take advantage of a hired man who is poor and needy, whether he is a brother Israelite or an alien living in one of your towns. Pay him his wages each day before sunset, because he is poor and is counting on it. Otherwise he may cry to the Lord against you, and you will be guilty of sin." And by "alien," Feuerstein emphasized, "they meant all people, all faiths, all races." Perhaps Feuerstein was thinking about the generations of immigrants to America who had supported their families through work at Malden Mills.

One newspaper columnist wrote that, as a boy, Aaron had actually questioned his grandfather's pay-disbursal system, wondering if this departure from standard American business practices was really necessary: "Young Aaron consulted his rabbi, who happened to be his maternal grandfather. His other grandfather, he was told, was right. In Leviticus, it is written, 'You are not permitted to oppress the working man because he is poor and needy.' Aaron memorized the passage in Hebrew—and lives by it."

As for the specific decisions he made after the Malden Mills fire, Feuerstein has repeatedly cited Hebrew teachings as his inspiration—for example, these two famous quotations from the first-century scholar Hillel: "In a situation where there is no righteous person, try to be a righteous person" and "Not all who increase their wealth are wise." Sayings like these were the guiding stars by which Feuerstein steered his company during the dark days of 1995.

No wonder Feuerstein's life and work are now being used by some religious teachers to illustrate the crucial Jewish concept of *tzedaka.*

This term is usually translated as "charity," but it means more than what the English word usually implies. *Tzedaka* comes from the word *tzedek,* which means "justice." Thus, in the Hebrew tradition, charitable giving is seen not merely as an act of kindness prompted by love or generosity. It is also an act of justice that fulfills our innate sense of what is fit and proper. Therefore, withholding *tzedaka* is not merely selfish and ignoble, it is literally a crime, a violation of one of the most important obligations in the life of a Jew. Hence the Talmudic saying, "*Tzedaka* is equal to all the other commandments combined." And hence, too, the requirement stated in Deuteronomy—and widely practiced in Jewish communities throughout history—that Jews should give a specified percentage of their incomes, such as 10 percent, to help the needy. Such a donation is not a mere free-will gift—it is demanded by the sense of justice embodied in our faith.

This concept of *tzedaka* as a social obligation to our fellow humans underlay the difficult, some would say self-sacrificing, choices that Aaron Feuerstein made. Because he viewed the workers at his textile plant as his equals in the eyes of God—as, of course, they are—Feuerstein had no other option than to do what he could to keep them whole, to prevent them and their families from suffering privation as a result of the tragic fire.

And because he was deeply rooted in a lifetime of Jewish practice, worship, study, and prayer, the notion of doing what was easy and self-serving—simply pocketing the insurance payments—never even occurred to him. As Feuerstein remarked when a reporter asked about the money, "And what would I do with it? Eat more? Buy another suit? Retire and die? No, that did not go into my mind."

Aaron Feuerstein represents the best in American business. But he also represents Jewish morality in action—the behavior of a mensch in those challenging moments when life confronts us with the choice between what is expedient and what is right. Many of those who know about his ethical example consider him a hero for our times. And as later chapters in this book will make clear, Feuerstein's ethically grounded approach to business decisions places him squarely at the heart of Jewish tradition. Among the world's great religions, Judaism is the one that places the greatest emphasis on moral behavior in relation to money—a fact that most non-Jews have never been taught.

Unfortunately, not everyone chooses to follow the ethical path that Aaron Feuerstein has walked.

Feuerstein's dark counterpart in the business arena may be another man who has garnered far more publicity and attention for his very different behavior—the fraudulent investment manager Bernard Madoff.

The outlines of the Madoff saga are well known—in fact, judging by the volume of coverage his case received, probably far more widely known than the heroic story of Aaron Feuerstein. And this disparity itself is one reason why I find the contrasting stories of Feuerstein and Madoff so revealing.

Born in Queens, New York, in 1938, Bernard Madoff graduated from Hofstra College in 1960, and in the same year founded Bernard L. Madoff Investment Securities LLC. Beginning as a penny-stock trader, Madoff gradually developed a wide-ranging network of clients for whom he bought and sold stocks as well as providing investment advice. His company also developed innovative computer technology to disseminate stock prices, which helped lead to the creation of the automated stock-trading system known as NASDAQ. In time, Madoff become a prominent leader among NASDAQ dealers, even serving as the organization's non-executive chairman. He also developed extensive personal ties among government regulators of the financial markets, ties that many say helped him avoid close scrutiny when questions were raised about his company's practices.

As Madoff's company prospered and expanded, his wife, Ruth, who had formerly worked at the New York Stock Exchange, became an employee of Madoff Securities, along with several other family members, including Madoff's two sons, his brother, a niece, and a nephew. For more than forty years, Madoff cultivated a reputation as an outstanding citizen and an astute businessman. So exceptional were the financial returns reported on Madoff's accounts that the number of individuals and institutions vying to become his clients grew steadily. Well-known organizations, including universities and nonprofits, gave Madoff Securities portions of their endowments to manage; in prominent social circles, Madoff clients bragged about their financial success and considered themselves lucky to be among the favored circle of people who benefited from Madoff's talents.

All in all, it was the image of a charmed life—a dedicated family man, an industry leader, a consummate professional—until the whole thing was exposed as a horrendous fraud.

It happened in December 2008, in the midst of the most serious financial and economic crisis since the Great Depression of the 1930s. Under increasing financial pressure, Madoff had been finding it more and more difficult to maintain the façade of success and prosperity he had nurtured for so long. Using the techniques of the classic Ponzi scheme, his company had been distributing funds from new investors to older clients, identifying them as "profits" on investment accounts. But as we now know, the profits weren't real because in most accounts there were *no* investments at all. The money had been used to pay fake dividends to other victims and also to support Bernard Madoff's lavish lifestyle—including his homes in Manhattan, Montauk, Palm Beach, and southern France—while Madoff shuffled cash around and doctored financial reports in an increasingly desperate effort to hide what was happening.

By the first week of December, with the stock market reeling from the global financial meltdown, Madoff's Ponzi scheme was collapsing. He confessed to his sons not only that he didn't have the money to cover some $7 billion in redemptions requested by anxious clients, but also that the entire business had been run in a fraudulent manner for years. It was "just one big lie," he told them. Madoff's sons reported the confession to federal authorities, and by December 11, Madoff was under arrest. Almost $65 billion supposedly held in client accounts, including both actual investment funds and fabricated gains, had disappeared.

In the months to come, the name Bernard Madoff, formerly known only to a relatively select community of financial professionals and well-heeled investors, would become a staple of the tabloids, cable news shows, blogs, and gossip magazines. Madoff came to symbolize much more than his own crimes. The collapse of huge, once highly respected financial institutions under the weight of excessive risk taking and debt; the irresponsibility of investors who sought high returns without questioning their source or their sustainability; the failure of regulators and the media to investigate or challenge apparently impossible tales of financial success; and the hubris and sense of entitlement seemingly felt by many of the most privileged in society—all of these came to be associated with the name and face of Bernard Madoff.

By June 29, 2009, when Madoff was sentenced to the maximum possible term of 150 years in prison on multiple counts of fraud and perjury, he had become one of the world's most famous—and most hated—individuals.

The rise, fall, and disgrace of Bernard Madoff is like something out of Greek drama—the tragic tale that has happened countless times in history and that, sadly, will happen again as long as greed, dishonesty, and gullibility remain weaknesses of human character. And at a time when millions of ordinary investors were watching their savings dwindle under the impact of the financial meltdown of 2008–2009, it was probably inevitable that the spectacular tale of

Bernie Madoff, replete with celebrity victims and page-six lifestyles, should capture the world's attention as the embodiment of all that's worst in the world of high finance.

Far more disturbing, however, is another aspect of the Madoff saga. I'm referring to the way in which Bernard Madoff has, for many people, come to symbolize not just the dangers of greed and dishonesty, but something much more specific, questionable, and troubling—namely, the supposed role of the Jew in the world of money.

Because, yes, Bernard Madoff—like Aaron Feuerstein—happens to be Jewish. He was raised in a Jewish family, married a Jewish woman, and socialized among a largely Jewish set of friends in New York and Florida. He was chairman of the board of directors of the business school of Yeshiva University, a historically Jewish institution, and served on the executive council of the Wall Street division of the United Jewish Appeal. And although many of the charities and foundations for whom Madoff invested funds were secular or nonsectarian, some were associated with specifically Jewish causes—for example, the Robert I. Lappin Charitable Foundation, which funds teen trips to Israel and development programs for Jewish educators.

There's no evidence that Madoff read the Torah nightly or devoted himself to ethical study as Aaron Feuerstein did. In that sense (and leaving aside the evidence of their respective business behaviors), we might assume that Feuerstein is more personally devoted to Jewish tradition and teachings than Madoff. But there's no denying that, in ethnic, social, and cultural terms, Bernard Madoff is Jewish—just like Aaron Feuerstein.

And unfortunately, Madoff's "Jewishness" became, for some people, the central story of the Madoff scandal.

At the Anti-Defamation League (ADL), one of our jobs is to monitor signs of evolving attitudes among religious, ethnic, and racial groups. We're among the leaders in the historic struggle against bigotry, intolerance, discrimination, and hatred based on creed, color, or heritage. When stories or controversies are in the news that have an obvious potential to arouse intergroup hostilities, we make it our business to trace their impact on society and report what we find. These days, that involves keeping tabs on an enormous range of formal and informal communications media, from mainstream newspapers, magazines, TV networks, and radio stations to little-known publications disseminated by fringe organizations and political groups, as well as the burgeoning world of the Internet.

In the wake of the Bernard Madoff scandal, we knew we would see an outpouring of rage against this man whose criminal behavior had harmed so many innocent victims—and indeed we did. But we wondered how much of that rage would focus on Madoff's ethnic and religious heritage. Would the fact that Madoff is Jewish be used as an excuse to attack *all* Jews by people who take it as their mission in life to foment bigotry and hatred?

The intolerant ones did not pass up this opportunity.

During the months between Madoff's arrest and his sentencing, we saw an incredible flood of anti-Semitic comments on mainstream and extremist Web sites. Hundreds of news sites, blogs, and financial message boards that ran stories about the Madoff scandal were inundated with responses that focused not on the villainy of one man but on the supposed propensity of all Jews to commit fraud in pursuit of profit. Popular news sites in New York and Florida—the two epicenters of the Madoff story—carried many anti-Semitic posts. Anti-Jewish postings could be found on many high-traffic news sites. At some sites, such as the online version of the *Palm Beach Post* newspaper, administrators were so appalled by the outpouring of vitriol that they decided to delete dozens of hate-filled screeds that had filled the normally unedited comments sections.

If you're wondering whether our characterization of these comments as anti-Semitic may be exaggerated or overly sensitive, we invite you to judge for yourself. Here are just a handful of typical examples from online news sites (with errors in grammar and spelling left unchanged):

> "Ho hum, another Crooked Wall Street Jew. Find a Jew who isn't Crooked. Now that would be a story."

> "One Jew thief robs another bunch of Jew thieves—I suppose that's what you'd call a victimless crime. I suppose if

he'd not scre*ed his fellow Jews—and robbed us poor gentiles it would've been absolutely kosher, eh?"

"Just another jew money changer thief. It's been happening for 3,000 years. Trust a Jew and this is what will happen. History has proven it over and over. Jews have only one god—money."

"This is simply the biggest jew to get caught swindling money. What about the thousands of other jews who do the same every day? What about the entire state of Israel that lies to, cheats and steals from the world? Madoff is just an example of a larger problem and the inherent, central element in jew culture."

"How many 'isolated incidents' regarding Wall Street shysters and financial crooks of all stripes does it take to establish the fact of Jewish greed? How many on the planet, even reputable Jews, have been defrauded and victimized by Jewish greed? How many could tell of their own experiences of being duped, lied to, conned and ripped-off by unscrupulous Jews? Tens of millions? More?"

Comments like these popped up not merely on far-right Web sites or those associated with hate groups. The Madoff story seemed to give bigots license to share their ignorant attitudes even in otherwise respectable venues. Perhaps they felt encouraged by the continual references by reporters and commentators to Madoff's religious background.

For example, on Forbes.com (the site maintained by the well-known financial magazine), columnist Philip Delves Broughton wrote about "Madoff's Money," summarizing the scam and noting, "So consistent were his returns in good times or bad, an investment in Madoff came to be called the 'Jewish Bond.'" That was enough to evoke reader comments in which the anti-Semitism was thinly veiled, such as "Has anyone looked for this money in Israel? It's where Lansky tried to stash his cash" and "Serves the greedy sheckel mongers for putting gold ahead of morality and God."

On the highly popular news-and-commentary Web site *The Huffington Post*, a story by journalist Laurence Leamer about the impact of Madoff's fraud on the Palm Beach crowd of affluent, largely Jewish investors evoked this comment: "It's harsh to say . . . but I have absolutely no sympathy at all for these people. They are greedy, have absolutely no regard or appreciation for the country that saved them from extinction and worst of all have an unspoken contempt for 'goyem.' The fascinating irony of this pathetic episode is they experienced a 'financial holocaust' by one of their own. Certainly something for them to ponder in sunny Palm Beach."

The online version of a story in the British newspaper the *Guardian* by journalist Richard Silverstein about the charities harmed by Madoff drew comments like these: "Oh come on . . . as if this is the first time someone in the Jewish community has been outed as a terrible and predatory criminal. You seem to be overlooking some fine gentlemen . . . like Louis Lepke, Dutch Schultz, Bugsy Siegel and Meyer Lansky, all of them fine and upstanding members of the Jewish-American community... not" and "Well, at least that's a few million less that can be spent on funding Israeli 'settlers" continuing theft of Arab land in the West Bank."

And so a pattern was established: A respectable outlet of the mainstream media would publish an article covering the Madoff case, which was undoubtedly an important and newsworthy story. But the article would often place an unusual degree of emphasis on the religious heritage of both the criminal and his victims, thereby eliciting an outpouring of anti-Semitic sentiments from people who appeared eager to seize any excuse for a diatribe against "the Jews."

Was Bernie Madoff Jewish? Undoubtedly. But was his faith the single most salient fact about him? Judging by the news coverage of his story, you might think so.

A profile of the scamster in the *New York Post* played the "Jewish angle" for all it was worth:

> Working the so-called "Jewish circuit" of well-heeled Jews he met at country clubs on Long Island and in Palm Beach, and through his position on the boards of directors of several prominent Jewish institutions, [Madoff] was entrusted with entire family fortunes.
>
> "The guy was totally respected. He was a *heymishe* Jewish guy. He had sweet old ladies and he let their children in," said a Manhattan lawyer who invested with Madoff.
>
> "This guy was dealing with all the rich Jews in Roslyn and the rich Jews in Palm Beach. This was passed down from

family member to family member because he wouldn't open up to new people."

Similarly, a profile of Madoff published in the *New York Times* just two days after his arrest ("Standing Accused: A Pillar of Finance and Charity") managed to use the word "Jewish" three times in its first nine paragraphs.

You might assume that this is standard journalistic practice—that the religious background of a newsworthy individual is always deemed a significant aspect of their life story. But a little research shows that's simply not so.

Consider one obvious comparison. Just a few weeks after the Madoff scandal broke, a similar story emerged about another high-profile financier accused of multi-billion-dollar fraud. The case was that of Robert Allen Stanford, founder of an offshore investment empire based in the island nation of Antigua. On February 21, 2009, the *Times* ran a lengthy profile of Stanford ("Fraud Case Shakes a Billionaire's Caribbean Realm") following virtually the same format as its story about Madoff.

It so happens that Stanford is not Jewish. (If it matters, it appears he is a Southern Baptist.) How often was Stanford's religion mentioned in the 41-paragraph article? You guessed it—zero times.

Were the editors of all these mainstream publications, from the *Times* and the *Post* to *Forbes* and the *Guardian,* deliberately courting anti-Semitic sentiment by publishing stories that emphasized Bernie Madoff's religion? I strongly doubt it. But did their coverage of the Madoff saga, along with that found in hundreds of other media outlets, whether print, broadcast, or Internet, have the effect of encouraging people to focus on Madoff's religion as if it had some direct connection with his crimes? I'm afraid it did.

When it comes to Jews and money, there are all too many who are ready to consider any bad news a form of good news—because it provides an excuse for anti-Semitism.

These two stories—the story of Aaron Feuerstein and the story of Bernard Madoff—are not directly related. But a comparison of the ways these stories have been covered in the mainstream media reveals something important—and disturbing—about our society and its attitudes.

In the case of Aaron Feuerstein, one of the most unusual and admirable business figures of our time, his religious heritage was treated, in most media coverage, as an interesting but distinctly secondary theme—despite the fact that being a devout Jew profoundly shaped the very ethical behavior that made Feuerstein newsworthy in the first place.

By contrast, in the case of Bernard Madoff, story after story emphasized his Jewish background—despite the fact that it was basically irrelevant to the history of fraud and deception that placed Madoff in the spotlight (just as Robert Allen Stanford's religion had nothing to do with his criminal activities).

Why this difference? I don't believe most of the writers and editors who covered these two stories had any religious or ethnic animus toward Jews. But I do think it's easy for all of us—including media professionals who should be especially sensitive to this danger—to fall back on familiar images, themes, and stereotypes. It's a form of lazy thinking that is difficult to avoid, especially when society is so deeply permeated by a particular pattern of ideas that many people aren't even fully aware of its ubiquity. And the pattern of stereotypes that the Madoff story activated in the minds of many people is a particularly deep-seated and pernicious one—the age-old pattern of false and slanderous beliefs about Jews and money.

With the United States and the world still struggling to overcome the impact of what many have called the Great Recession of 2008–2009, this is an especially dangerous time for these bigoted beliefs to reemerge.

In times of social stress or economic hardship, the search for scapegoats tends to intensify. During the Great Depression of the 1930s, this response was exemplified in the United States by bigots like Father Coughlin, the anti-Semitic broadcaster whom some have called "the father of hate radio"—and far more tragically in Europe by the rise of the Nazis.

During the last great economic upheaval in the 1980s, many commentators flirted with anti-Semitism when analyzing the crimes of financiers like Michael Milken and Ivan Boesky. For example, the most famous book about the scandals of that era, *Den of Thieves* by James B. Stewart, has a title that recalls the words of Jesus—"It is written, My house shall be called the house of prayer; but ye have made it a den of thieves," from Matthew 21:13—often used by anti-Semites to associate Christ with their own belief that Jews are inherently greedy and dishonest.

So when the financial crisis erupted in the fall of 2008, concerns arose about possible anti-Semitic reactions. In the Jewish community, and in particular at the ADL, our antennae were up. One of the most prominent, persistent, and entrenched elements of anti-Semitism is the network of beliefs surrounding Jews and money—beliefs like "Jews are greedy," "Jews own Wall Street," "Jews run the banks," "Jews care only about money," "Jews will do anything to increase their own wealth," "Jews believe it's okay to defraud non-Jews," and even "Jewish tentacles control world capitalism and manipulate it for their own benefit." Whenever the financial world experiences upheaval, many in the Jewish community worry that Jews will be assigned the blame.

Sure enough, as the economic and financial crisis of 2008–2009 began to dominate the news and take a toll on the personal circumstances of millions of people, blame-the-Jews statements erupted on the Internet and in traditional media. Blogs and chatrooms on mainstream financial Web sites and elsewhere were bombarded with anti-Semitic comments and others that flirted with anti-Semitism. A few of the hundreds of samples the ADL collected:

> "World-Jewry Finance grabbled trillions of Euro's and Dollars. Among them the Jews, Rothschild and Morgan-Stanley. With the trillions they will incite further wars and finance them." . . . "Jews have infiltrated Wall Street and Government and have ruined our country." . . . "Can you see why the Jews need to be routed out and sent packing? . . . They are a cancer on our society."

Beliefs like these have widespread international currency. Thus, in September 2008, Iranian president Mahmoud Ahmadinejad told the gathering of world leaders at the United Nations General Assembly that Zionists, although they are a small minority, "have been dominating an important portion of the financial and monetary centers . . . in a deceitful, complex and furtive manner."

This is the bigger background that makes a story like that of Bernard Madoff, and its treatment by the media and the general public, an important bellwether—not because of its inherent significance, but as a barometer of how social and economic stresses are affecting the fabric of civility and mutual tolerance that groups like ADL and many others have fought to create and protect for generations.

All of this would be disturbing enough. But three particular factors require us to take this problem especially seriously today.

First, there has been much talk in recent years about how anti-Semitism has changed, with many saying that events in Israel and the struggle for peace in the Middle East have become the new focus of anti-Jewish bigotry. But the anti-Semitism expressed in these revived canards about Jews and money is not some "new" anti-Semitism but rather the "classic" anti-Semitism that has caused such damage and destruction to the Jewish people. Accusing Jews of being responsible for the woes of mankind through their conspiratorial control of the worldwide financial system is an age-old slander that can be traced back at least to the discredited nineteenth-century forgery, the so-called *Protocols of the Learned Elders of Zion*. Seeing it winning new converts in the twenty-first century is disheartening, to say the least.

A second worrisome factor is that these accusations come in the context of a period of resurgence of related anti-Semitic conspiracy theories around the world that have infiltrated the mainstream.

Since the 9/11 terrorist attacks, a series of weird charges against Jews have surfaced that are believed by millions of people the world over: that Jews and Israel were responsible for the attacks, not Osama bin Laden and al-Qaeda; that the United States was dragged into the war in Iraq by American Jews to serve Israel's interests; and that the Holocaust is a myth fabricated by Jews to promote a sinister agenda—specifically, the control of the Middle East and the manipulation of U.S. foreign policy for the benefit of the Jews. Add to these beliefs the notion that Jews have some kind of special, secret, and self-serving relationship to money and world business, and you have a cocktail of ideas whose virulence resembles that of the traditional anti-Semitic fantasies that led to millions of deaths over the last two millennia.

The third compelling factor is the power of the Internet as a worldwide communications medium with no filters or controls. With all its huge benefits, the Internet is also a unique instrument for spreading hate. So when the financial crisis and the Madoff scandal generate waves of anti-Semitism on the Internet, there's cause for concern among all those who want to build a more tolerant, just, and peaceful world.

All these reasons help to explain why what one might call "the Bernie Madoff moment" really matters. In a time of global economic crisis, the time is ripe for a careful, detailed examination of the age-old lies about money and the Jews—the origins of these beliefs, their tenuous relationship to historical realities, the social and psychological functions they serve, their destructive impact on all humankind, and the appropriate response from people of good will.

It's sad to realize that anti-Semitism is not merely a history lesson—it's a current event. But knowledge and understanding are the antidotes to ignorance and hatred. It's time to explode, once and for all, the bigoted beliefs and attitudes about Jews and money that have infected even the minds and hearts of many well-intentioned people. In the subsequent chapters of this book, I'll do just that.

2
THE STORY
OF A
STEREOTYPE

n one form or another, anti-Semitism has bedeviled humanity for almost as long as the Jewish people have existed. It arose prior to the modern phenomenon of racism—that is, hatred or prejudice based on real or perceived racial identity—which many scholars have noted did not really exist in the ancient world or even in early Christian times. Anti-Semitism seems to have predated even the theological rivalries among the world's three great monotheistic faiths—Judaism, Christianity, and Islam. It obviously existed long before the economic system we call capitalism, which means that the peculiar strain of anti-Semitism that focuses on false beliefs about the excessive power of Jews in the marketplace must be viewed as simply one thread, and not the oldest, in a complicated tapestry of hate.

Tracing the roots of anti-Semitism is complicated, and a full examination of the topic is beyond the scope of this book. But a brief description of the origin of anti-Semitism is important if we are to understand how the myths surrounding Jews and money have come to be.

Although anti-Semitism did not assume its fullest and most destructive form until Christian times, it was foreshadowed in earlier periods. In pre-Christian times, anti-Jewish sentiments and behaviors may have been simply one form of the intertribal conflicts in which practically all the peoples of Eurasia were variously embroiled. Traces of such conflicts can still be seen in the Hebrew scriptures—for example, in this passage from the biblical Book of Esther (3:8–9), in which we see Haman, an advisor to the Persian king, proposing what amounts to an ancient version of a pogrom:

> And Haman said unto King Ahasuerus, "There is a certain nation scattered abroad and dispersed among the peoples in all the provinces of thy kingdom; and their laws are diverse from those of every people; neither keep they the king's laws; therefore it profiteth not the king to suffer them. If it please the king, let it be written that they be destroyed; and I will pay ten thousand talents of silver into the hands of those that have the charge of the king's business, to bring it into the king's treasuries."

In the words of Haman, we encounter many of the familiar elements of anti-Semitism: the distrust of Jews as an alien people, dispersed among those of other nations yet keeping their own set of rules and customs; the sense that these aliens are disloyal and not to be trusted; and the readiness to regard the Jews as dispensable. (The rest of the biblical book, of course, recounts how the heroic Queen Esther saved the Jews from destruction by Haman's intended attack, a deliverance still celebrated in the holiday of Purim.)

The causes of this distrust of the Jews aren't hard to find. In the pagan world of the Middle East and the Mediterranean, the monotheism of the Jews and their adherence to a strict code of moral, ethical, and devotional conduct set them apart from other peoples in ways that led, perhaps inevitably, to conflict and suspicion. In the great cities of the Greek and Roman empires, for example, people of many nations mingled freely, and temples to gods from various cultures could be found side by side. Generally speaking, these varied cults lived in an atmosphere of mutual acceptance, the unspoken assumption being that your god is yours, my god is mine, and both are equally real. Often, all citizens were expected to pay taxes to support the upkeep of pagan temples, including those in which they did not personally worship.

Only the Jews took a different attitude. Divine revelation as recounted in Hebrew scripture had taught them that there was only one God; they refused to acknowledge the existence of any other gods or to pay tribute to them, financially or otherwise. Combined with the distinctive customs and religious practices of the Jews—their dietary laws, for example, as well as their reluctance to intermarry—this insistence on the exclusive authority of their own faith made the Jews appear to be a people apart who considered themselves "better" than their neighbors. As a result, they were subject to distrust and sometimes hatred.

It was not until the rise of Christianity, however, that anti-Semitism began to take on its tragic modern proportions. Of course, the founder of the Christian faith, Jesus of Nazareth, was himself a Jew, as were his earliest followers. Jesus was immersed in Jewish teaching and regarded himself as another in the line of Jewish sages and prophets, not as the founder of a new faith.

After Jesus's death (and, in Christian teaching, his resurrection and ascent to heaven), the community his followers established began to develop in unexpected ways. Although some of the Jews of ancient Palestine joined the new sect devoted to Jesus, most did not. Jesus's followers began to preach and teach among the gentiles, and they gradually spread the Christian teachings in Greece, Italy, Asia Minor, and elsewhere in the Mediterranean world. Soon the majority of Christians came from non-Jewish ethnic and cultural backgrounds, and the church gradually shed its original identity as a branch of Judaism.

The Christian Bible itself reflects this process. For example, chapter 11 of the Acts of the Apostles recounts a vision supposedly experienced by Peter, the preeminent leader of the early church, in which a divine messenger releases the Christians from the obligation to follow Jewish dietary laws, thereby resolving one longstanding conflict between Jewish Christians (such as the apostle Paul) and gentile Christians (such as Peter) in favor of the gentile contingent. Though couched as a heavenly revelation, this vision can also be interpreted as a reflection of social, political, and demographic trends in early Christianity, with growing numbers of non-Jewish converts gradually displacing Jews from positions of dominance in the new religion.

In time, of course, Christianity became the dominant faith of Europe and the Mediterranean world. Its political ascendancy was ratified in the fourth century C.E. with the conversion of the Roman emperor Constantine, who made Christianity the official religion of the empire. As a result, the same imperial power that had previously been used to suppress Christianity (as well as Judaism) now set about converting the entire population of Europe to Christianity—willingly if possible, by force if necessary.

For the next millennium, the Jews of Europe occupied a peculiar position. Those who refused to convert to Christianity became a tiny religious minority in a culture in which church and state were practically one. Having failed to accept the only faith that the broader society deemed legitimate, they were themselves rejected, the ultimate outsiders. Yet it was always understood that Christianity was in some sense a descendant of Judaism. The roots of Jesus's teaching in Jewish scripture were too obvious to ignore, and the Hebrew Bible was itself incorporated into the Christian Bible. How would the newly empowered Christians reconcile this duality—that while Christianity was supposed to have a monopoly on religious truth, Judaism was, spiritually speaking, the elder sibling?

In response to this contradiction, Christianity developed a set of doctrines that ultimately established one of the three pillars of modern anti-Semitism—the accusation of deicide.

First, in order to establish the primacy of Christianity, it was necessary for Christians to discard the traditional scriptural identification of the Jews as being the chosen people of God. Christian theologians did so, declaring that God had rejected the Jews for their refusal to accept Jesus as the Savior. In their place, God had elevated the Christians into the role of the "the new Israel," as if the older sibling had proven disappointing to his father and therefore been disinherited in favor of the younger son.

In Christian eyes, it was bad enough that the Jews had rejected Jesus. Far worse, however, was the notion that the Jews were responsible for his death on the cross. This accusation of deicide—God-murder—was first explicitly lodged against the Jews by Bishop Melito of Sardis as far back as the second century C.E. Gradually it spread through Christian circles until it became the dominant interpretation of the death of Jesus. In this version of the Gospel story, the crucial roles in the crucifixion of Christ are played by Judas, the disloyal apostle who betrays Jesus in return for thirty pieces of silver, and by the Jewish crowds in Jerusalem who demand the death of Jesus (having been encouraged to do so by their chief priests and elders).

The falsehood of this charge has long been clear to unbiased inquirers. Over the last century, scholars studying the historical record, including common political, judicial, and religious practices in first-century Palestine, have demonstrated that the execution of

Jesus was instigated not by the Jewish people but by the Roman authorities who ruled Palestine in the first century C.E. Those Roman rulers viewed Jesus as one in a long line of rabble-rousing prophets and teachers who posed a threat to peace and stability in the region. Thus, the anti-Jewish rhetoric that mars several books of the Christian New Testament has been shown to reflect not historical fact but the rivalry between Jews who followed Jesus and those who did not at the time the books were written. That means that the rhetoric actually predates the formal separation between what we now call Christianity and its source, Judaism.

Nonetheless, versions of the Gospel narratives that emphasized Jewish guilt rather than the responsibility of the Roman imperial authorities who actually imposed and carried out the death sentence came to be included in the Christian Bible. As a result, with every annual reading or reenactment of the story of the death of Jesus in Christian churches, millions of Christians imbibed the notion that the Jews had been guilty of the worst crime in history. This recirculation of libel against an entire people has continued into our own time in thoughtless and inaccurate Easter pageants, passion plays, and dramatic depictions of the last days of Jesus, including, for example, Mel Gibson's controversial (and unfortunately extremely popular) 2004 film *The Passion of the Christ.* The deicide libel has been used to justify hatred of Jews and violence against them—including from Christian pulpits. Through the centuries, these denunciations have led to countless outbreaks of violence against Jews, including murderous pogroms—a bitterly ironic celebration of the legacy of the man Christians revere as "the Prince of Peace."

Once the accusation of deicide was in place, Christian anti-Semitism became a psychological juggernaut that would drive two millennia of tragic history. Scholars like the late James Parkes have traced a direct line from ancient Christian teachings on Jews and Judaism to Hitler's death camps.

The theological labeling of Jews as "Christ-killers," then, is the first historic pillar of anti-Semitism. The second, which is powerfully supported and reinforced by the first, is the suspicion of Jewish disloyalty—the belief that the Jews who live as a distinct minority in countries and cultures around the world constitute a kind of secret society of would-be traitors whose only true loyalty is to one another, not to the larger society in which they move.

As suggested by the passage from the Book of Esther quoted earlier, this branding of Jews as dangerous outsiders can be traced deep into history. But it reached a pinnacle during the medieval and Renaissance periods in Christian Europe and the Muslim Near East.

Given the close ties between civil and religious authorities throughout these centuries, it was inevitable that anti-Jewish doctrines would ultimately be reflected in political and economic restrictions on Jews. That's exactly what happened. The medieval re-pression of the Jews throughout Christendom reached a climax in the Fourth Lateran Council of 1215, which for the first time pre-scribed distinctive dress for the Jews of Europe (to isolate and stig-matize them), banned them from public office, and even subjected them to a special tax to be paid to Christian clergy.

Reinforcing these legal restrictions was what scholar George M. Frederickson has described as "a folk mythology" that "put Jews out-side the pale of humanity by literally demonizing them." Jews were accused of bizarre crimes that supposedly echoed their original murder of Jesus—for example, the crucifixion of Christian children and the use of Christian blood in devilish secret ceremonies. In communities all over Europe, Jews were regarded as in league with Satan, practitioners of witchcraft, fomenters of heresy, and a danger-ous threat to the safety of any town or village where they resided.

Other manifestations of this virulent anti-Semitism in the Chris-tian Europe of the Middle Ages and the Renaissance include the blaming of Jewish saboteurs for the supposedly deliberate spreading of the Black Plague that decimated Europe in the fourteenth century; the torture and killing of Jews (and other heretics) under the Inquisi-tion by Torquemada in Spain during the fifteenth century as well as by other inquisitors before and after him; the expulsion of the Jews from England in 1290 and from Spain in 1492; and the papal bull *Cum Nimis Absurdum,* issued by Pope Paul IV in 1555, that barred

Jews from owning real estate, attending Christian universities, hiring Christian servants, and engaging freely in commerce.

Of course, the accusation that Jews constituted an alien "fifth column" within Christendom had a self-fulfilling quality. The more thoroughly Jews were excluded from mainstream society by legal, religious, and social attacks, the more separate and distinctive would they appear to the Christian majority—and therefore the more highly suspect. Codes that discriminated against Jews and erected barriers between them and their Christian neighbors inevitably made the Jews seem increasingly "foreign" in their own communities, which in turn deepened the mistrust and fear they engendered.

It's sometimes said that, in the medieval and Renaissance periods, the Islamic nations of the Middle East were far more hospitable to Jews than the countries of Christendom. There's some truth to this idea. For example, during the period of Islamic rule in Spain, a sizable Jewish community existed and flourished, and Jewish scholars made notable contributions to Iberian philosophy and science. Virulent anti-Semitic sentiment was not as widespread in Muslim societies as in Christian ones. But Jews were subject to discriminatory statutes and sometimes mistreatment. Classified as *dhimmi,* or non-Muslim, Jews were permitted to practice their faith but were required to pay a special tax (the *jizya*) from which Muslims were exempt. They could not testify in a court of law, and in some Muslim communities they were required to wear distinctive garb, to live in particular neighborhoods, and to practice only prescribed occupations. Pressure on Jews to convert to Islam varied from mild to intense.

In short, there's no doubt that Jews were considered outsiders in the nations of Islam, just as they were in Christian Europe. And as history has shown repeatedly, anyone considered a social outsider is never completely safe, especially in times of social stress or turmoil.

Today, legal restrictions on the freedom of Jews have disappeared from the Western world (though not from some Muslim countries). Yet the suspicion that Jews are outsiders whose loyalty and trustworthiness is questionable lingers on. Perhaps its strongest overt form today is the recurrent accusation that Jews in the United States and other countries are really loyal only to Israel and to their fellow Jews. Much of the controversy over the supposed power of the Israel lobby in American (and, to a lesser extent, European) politics represents a veiled form of this charge. Its not-so-subtle implication is that Jewish Americans would be happy to sacrifice the best interests, and even perhaps the security, of the United States if this would benefit Israel.

And this brings us to the third pillar of traditional anti-Semitism—the belief in a special, sinister connection between Jews and money. This belief is linked with the first two pillars but also has its own complicated history.

Like the accusation of deicide, it has its roots in Christian tradition. As we noted earlier, during medieval times the New Testament story of Judas, the disciple who betrayed Jesus in exchange for thirty pieces of silver, became lodged in the minds of millions of Christians as a symbol of Jewish treachery motivated by greed. Other episodes from the Christian Bible have been used for the same purpose. For example, there is the story of Jesus driving the money changers out of the temple in Jerusalem, as recounted in Matthew 21:12–13: "And Jesus went into the temple of God, and cast out all them that sold and bought in the temple, and overthrew the tables of the money changers, and the seats of them that sold doves, and said unto them, It is written, My house shall be called the house of prayer; but ye have made it a den of thieves."

As we noted in chapter 1, that last phrase, "den of thieves," has been appropriated by anti-Semites as a code phrase to describe, and vilify, the supposedly nefarious business practices of the Jews. Actually, most scholars agree that the biblical story describes an event that would have taken place in the so-called Court of the Gentiles, where travelers from around the world, including non-Jews, would have exchanged money for the purpose of making sacrifices in the temple, a practice that would have been common in the highly tolerant Roman world. Jesus appears to have been incensed over the fact that some of the money changers may have charged too much for their services. The notion that he was condemning the Jewish people in general would never have occurred to him or to his contemporaries—but that hasn't stopped anti-Semites from pointing to this passage to create the impression that Jesus disavowed his own Jewish heritage.

Thus, there are traces as far back as the Christian Bible of today's anti-Semitic beliefs concerning Jews and money. Still, it's unlikely that the peculiar set of stereotypes now associated with this relationship would ever have come into existence had it not been for a number of specific events in European history. The most significant of these was the gradual exclusion, beginning in medieval times, of Jews from most traditional professions. By the thirteenth century, Jews were forbidden to own land in virtually all of Europe, which meant, in practice, that they were unable to take part in agriculture (which had been their chief occupation in biblical times). They were also increasingly barred from participation in crafts and manufacturing—for example, the Jews of southern Europe, who had pioneered techniques for the making of glass and paper, were gradually driven out of these businesses and displaced by Christian owners.

These restrictions left only a handful of occupations in which Jews could earn a living, all of them considered economically marginal in the feudal world of medieval Europe. One of these was commerce—the buying and selling of goods, often by traveling merchants who carried products from the region of their manufacture into other countries where they could be traded for local commodities. This was a business to which the Jews were well suited for historical reasons: Since their dispersion from the land of Israel, the Jews had become "the people of the diaspora," scattered across many countries, speaking various languages and adopting various cultural practices yet retaining family ties and, of course, their ancestral faith. Thus, many Jews had friends and family members spread out over a large part of the then-known world, which became the basis of trading networks connecting the Middle East with North Africa and the countries of Europe. We see a similar pattern in some of today's diaspora peoples—for example, the so-called overseas Chinese, who have used family ties to form very successful business networks connecting companies throughout the Pacific rim.

The other occupation open to the Jews was moneylending—the nascent business from which today's vast financial industries, including banking, are descended. Left with few options, the Jews of medieval Europe became merchants and moneylenders—and in time they became very skilled at both occupations.

So the association of Jews with moneylending came about because of these vagaries of history and the discrimination to which the Jews were subject even then. But over the centuries of the Middle Ages and Renaissance in Europe, the role of the moneylender became freighted with ethical problems that easily translated into a stain on the character of Jews. The restrictions suffered by the Jews that forced them into financial occupations also helped fuel fresh torrents of anti-Semitism. In the words of Heinrich Heine, the nineteenth-century German poet, himself a Jew, "In this way the Jews were legally condemned to be rich, hated, and murdered."

One of the ethical problems that helped foster anti-Jewish animus was the issue of usury. Both the Hebrew scriptures and the Christian New Testament contain passages that seem to flatly condemn the charging of interest on moneylending, often using the term "usury" to define that practice. For example, in Exodus 22:25 we read, "If you advance money to any poor man amongst my people, you shall not act like a moneylender: you must not exact interest in advance from him." Similarly, in Leviticus 25:35–37, we read, "When your brother-Israelite is reduced to poverty and cannot support himself in the community, you shall assist him. . . . You shall not deduct interest when advancing him money nor add interest to the payment due for food supplied on credit." And Psalm 15:5 says of the righteous man that he "does not put his money out to usury."

Based on these and other biblical proscriptions, the Christian church of the Middle Ages condemned usury, with the strongest anti-usury campaign beginning around the time of the Second Lateran Council of 1139. Christians who charged interest were subject to attack and punishment by church officials, including by the leaders of the Inquisition in the thirteenth century.

Yet this created a serious economic problem for medieval Europe. If lending money at interest is forbidden, where would necessary funds be found in times of need, or when investment capital is required to promote business growth? The notion of lending as pure charity may be appealing, and certainly it's appropriate under some circumstances, as when helping the poor during an emergency—but it's not a very practical prescription for economic development.

In response to this dilemma, the medieval church developed a convenient, if hypocritical, strategy: It quietly turned a blind eye to moneylending when practiced by non-Christian businesspeople, who were not subject to the restrictions established by the church's Canon Law. Thus, in practice, Jewish members of local communities were permitted if not encouraged to become the lenders-at-interest to whom Christians turned when in need. The all-but-spoken rationale seems to have been, "Since the Jews are condemned to hell anyway, they might as well commit one more sin—and provide the rest of us with a valuable service in the process!"

Were the Jews who became moneylenders at this time violating their own religion's teachings by charging interest? Not necessarily. Jewish thinking about this ethical question is complicated and many-sided. As quasi-modern economic systems began to develop in the Middle Ages, and the need for moneylending became economically important, Jewish law began to adapt to the new realities. One of the methods employed was the development of the legal fiction known as *heter iska,* or permission to do business, which entitles a lender to a set percentage of the future profits earned on the monies lent. A little thought makes it clear that this is the equivalent of interest, though not called by that name. Moses Maimonides, the great twelfth-century scholar, was one of many teachers who proposed simple ways around the biblical proscription on usury—for example, by having a loan repaid through a third party who would receive a slightly larger sum than the amount originally borrowed.

Eventually, under the pressure of economic realities, the restrictions on lending at interest were gradually eliminated throughout Europe. During the fourteenth, fifteenth, and sixteenth centuries, Christians took over the lucrative banking charters that Jews had once held. By the early modern period, the Jewish near-monopoly on financial occupations was gone. But the association of Jews with moneylending remained prominent in the minds of many Christians—and an important element of the current stereotyped image of Jews and money was firmly established.

One might think that the issue of usury is today a mere historical curiosity, living as we do in a modern world in which the charging and paying of interest are practically universal and generally accepted as crucial tools of economic growth and development. If modern finance—including interest—has made the modern world possible, then surely being associated with such finance should be a source of pride rather than shame for today's Jews.

Yet, the stigma attached to usury continues to have a certain emotional power, at least on the fringes of modern society. The great modernist poet Ezra Pound, whose literary genius did not prevent him from falling prey to strange political, social, and economic notions, devoted substantial sections of his masterwork *The Cantos* to an eloquent, vicious diatribe against interest-paying finance in which anti-Semitic slurs blend with nostalgia for an imagined "pure" world modeled on medieval Christendom from which the ills of contemporary life would supposedly be banished. In the writings of Pound and other antimodernist thinkers, the problems of the modern world are often blamed on the influence of the Jews. At times, we all dislike some aspects of contemporary life; anti-Semitism makes it easy to blame all those problems on a single group. The proposition that usury is at the root of modern economic woes gives this blame game a veneer of intellectual respectability.

On a different frontier of modern society, the contemporary Islamic world is also wrestling with the ethical dimensions of finance, including the issue of interest. Since sharia, Islamic law, continues to forbid the charging of interest, Islamic scholars and financial experts have developed a number of complex "work-arounds" that permit borrowing, lending, and investing while avoiding any practice that is overtly identifiable as interest. For example, rather than providing a mortgage loan at interest, an Islamic bank might buy the house from the homeowner and then resell it to him at a slightly higher price, payable over time. Today some 300 Islamic banks in 51 countries do business in accordance with such principles.

The fact that devout Muslims have developed an economic system that enables them to participate in modern business without violating their religious beliefs is, of course, understandable. But Islam's continuing condemnation of usury and the suspicion some Muslims direct toward Western institutions such as banks and investment companies remain an element in the widespread anti-Semitism in the Muslim world, since Muslims have borrowed from Christians the stereotyped though inaccurate image of the Jew as moneylender. We see this link in its most extreme form in terrorist Osama bin Laden's "Letter to America" from November 2002:

> You are the nation that permits Usury, which has been forbidden by all the religions. Yet you build your economy and investments on Usury. As a result of this, in all its different forms and guises, the Jews have taken control of your economy, through which they have then taken control of your media, and now control all aspects of your life making you their servants and achieving their aims at your expense.

The same stereotyped image of the Jew as usurer whose financial power gives him control over entire societies can be found not just in the writings of a fanatic like bin Laden but in editorials, cartoons, and news stories throughout the mainstream press of the Middle East.

The historical role of the Jews as financiers to the nations of Western Christendom fueled anti-Semitism in other ways. One is that specific Jewish financiers played important roles in facilitating the affairs of European ruling houses during the medieval and Renaissance periods. Jewish bankers operated only with royal permission, support, and implicit protection. In return, the profits earned by the moneylenders were subject to heavy taxes that often constituted an important source of royal income (and were sometimes supplemented by large and unavoidable bribes as well—with the implicit threat of religious persecution as punishment for any failure to pay up). Thus, a symbiotic relationship grew up between the Christian rulers and the Jewish financiers whose theoretically "sinful" services they relied upon. As historian H. H. Ben-Sasson has suggested, "One may almost refer to Jewish moneylenders as 'officials' of the Christian rulers." Similarly, scholar James Parkes has noted that the Jewish moneylenders "lived between the devil of royal extortion and the deep sea of ecclesiastical repression."

You might assume that their important role in the nation's economic life would win the Jews a modicum of respect, if not affection. But human psychology can be complicated, even perverse. A commonly seen example is that when we are dependent on someone else for anything important in life, our feelings toward that person can gradually become less and less appreciative and more and more resentful. This is especially likely to happen when the person we depend upon is viewed, for some reason, as being "the other" rather than one of us.

For a contemporary example, think about how the American public views the Arab nations on whom they depend for much of the oil that keeps their cars and factories running, or the Chinese investors and financiers who own increasing quantities of U.S. government debt. The more Americans feel beholden to foreigners, the more vulnerable they feel toward them—and the greater are the latent fear and hostility they also feel. It's not hard to imagine people in Western Europe, including those in the elite classes, feeling this same blend of vulnerability, fear, and hostility toward the Jews on whom they depended for financial services.

The Jewish moneylender may have played an important role in the creation of the modern world economy. But in the wake of dependency, very few Christians felt grateful for the help. Often, resentment, even hatred, was the dominant emotion that developed in the wake of this relationship.

And when this resentment became mingled with anti-Jewish religious sentiment, already a deep-rooted element of Christianity because of the historic rivalry between the two faiths and the resulting accusations of deicide and disloyalty, the result was historic episodes that are startling in their arbitrariness, cruelty, and viciousness. Thus, in 1349, when the Black Death swept Europe, it was blamed by many Christians on those familiar scapegoats, the Jews. And as one chronicler of the period, Jacob von Königshofen of Strasbourg, recorded, it was easy to use the stereotyped image of the Jews and financial exploiters to turn this crisis into an opportunity for violence and exploitation:

> On Saturday—that was St. Valentine's Day—they burnt the Jews on a wooden platform in their cemetery. There were about two thousand people of them. Those who wanted to baptize themselves were spared. Many small children were taken out of the fire and baptized against the will of their fathers and mothers. And everything that was owed to the Jews was cancelled, and the Jews had to surrender all pledges and notes that they had taken for debt. The council, however, took the cash that the Jews possessed and divided it among the workingmen proportionately. The money was indeed the thing that killed the Jews. If they had been poor and if the feudal lords had not been in debt to them, they would not have been burnt.

Maybe the most remarkable thing about this account is the honesty of those last two sentences in acknowledging the role that economic self-interest seems to have played in episodes of anti-Semitic violence like this one. It was indeed convenient for Christians to blame the Jews for all the evils of the world, as that provided a handy excuse to plunder them.

According to one major strain of scholarly thinking, even the notorious repression of the Spanish Inquisition may have been caused, in large part, by such economic self-interest. Historian Benzion Netanyahu has conducted perhaps the most extensive study of the Inquisition. He found that, in the Second Inquisition, the chief target of the Spanish authorities was not the *marranos*—the "secret Jews" who maintained their traditional religious practices while pretending adherence to Christianity—but rather the *conversos,* who actually converted to Christianity, usually under duress. This choice of target was strange, since, as Netanyahu explains, the *conversos* were faithful practitioners of their Christian faith and were guilty of neither deception nor heresy. What they *were* guilty of was rising social, political, and especially economic power, which produced enormous resentment among the Spanish people of every class. This resentment fueled the hostility and violence that led to the execution of some two thousand people between 1480 and 1530. Heresy may have been the excuse, but hostility toward Jews and money was the real motive.

Under pressure from the inherently unjust economic arrangements imposed by the authorities of most European nations, relationships between Christians and Jews became psychologically and socially warped. In this distorted atmosphere, rife with resentments, guilt, and hostility, the stereotype of the greedy Jew taking advantage of non-Jewish society took root and continues to flourish to this day. And, of course, the classic embodiment of this stereotype is the character of Shylock from Shakespeare's play *The Merchant of Venice*—written between 1596 and 1598, at the very cusp of the transition between the Renaissance and modern worlds—reflecting the shifting attitudes toward usury, commerce, and finance that still lead some people to have mixed feelings of envy, admiration, revulsion, and respect for the successful business person.

Over time, many variations on this stereotype have developed, some of which are mutually contradictory. There's the image of Jews as business geniuses whose values are centered entirely around the accumulation of money. Karl Marx, father of socialism, saw the Jews as the supreme exemplars of the capitalist spirit, when he wrote:

> What is the Jew's foundation in our world? Material necessity, private advantage.
> What is the object of the Jews' worship in this world? Usury/huckstering.
> What is his worldly god? Money. . . .
> Money is the zealous one god of Israel, beside which no other god may stand. Money degrades all the gods of mankind and turns them into commodities. Money is the universal and self-constituted value set upon all things. It has therefore robbed the whole world, of both nature and man, of its original value. Money is the essence of man's life and work, which have become alienated from him. This alien monster rules him and he worships it.

Karl Marx, incidentally, was not Jewish, though anti-Semites have "accused" him of this for generations. His father, Heinrich Marx, had been born a Jew but converted to Lutheranism before his son's birth, partly for social reasons, partly due to sincere conviction. Karl himself was baptized and raised as a Christian.

Decades later, though writing from a very different perspective and with admiration, economist John Maynard Keynes depicted the Jews as the world's greatest capitalists:

> Perhaps it is not an accident that the race which did most to bring the promise of immortality into the heart and essence of our religions has also done the most for the principle of compound interest and particularly loves this most purposive of human institutions.

In the 1920s, one of the world's greatest industrialists, automaker Henry Ford, made his vision of Jews as world-dominating capitalist manipulators into the center of an entire worldview. In his own newspaper, the *Dearborn Independent,* Ford ran a ninety-one-part series of articles under the title *The International Jew: The World's Problem,* which set forth the theory that the First World War had been instigated by a consortium of Jewish bankers eager to enrich themselves through the high-interest loans that European governments would take out to finance armament purchases.

Adolf Hitler himself was an admirer of *The International Jew,* and when the series was published in book form in German translation, it became a massive best-seller in Nazi Germany. Hitler particularly appreciated Ford's "analysis" of the conspiratorial role of the Jews in fomenting the First World War for their own economic benefit. He took it a step further, joining other Germans disheartened by their defeat in the war who blamed it not on any failure of the proud German army but rather on a home front "betrayal" by internal forces—Socialists, Communists, and especially the Jews. Not only had the Jews failed to support the German military as patriotic citizens should do—a claim that ignored the sizable Jewish participation in the war—they had, according to Hitler, undermined it through arms profiteering that sapped the army of badly needed resources.

This so-called stab-in-the-back legend had actually arisen during the war itself. Fueled by preexisting anti-Semitism, rumors swirled throughout Germany that Jewish citizens were shirking military service. In response, the German military high command had conducted an unprecedented Jewish census (*Judenzählung*) in November 1916, to determine the rate of Jewish participation in the war effort. To the embarrassment of the high command, the census proved that 80 percent of Jews had served on the front lines. (Subsequent studies have found that Jews had not only enlisted in higher percentages than non-Jews but also served in combat units and died at higher rates than their gentile counterparts.) The census results were not made public, supposedly to "spare Jewish feelings" but actually to conceal the foolishness of the assumptions that had driven it in the first place.

Despite being badly at odds with reality, the stab-in-the-back legend became the official Nazi theory concerning the war. It jibed nicely with the prevalent anti-Semitic beliefs: that Jews have no loyalty to any group other than themselves; that Jews are naturally treacherous; and that Jews will do anything for money. Hitler rode this legend, with its appealing mixture of self-exoneration and vicious scapegoating, into power at the head of a movement of bitter, discouraged, and angry German citizens.

Alongside Ford's image of Jews as international capitalist masters we find the image of Jews as secret communists using their wealth and influence to destroy liberty and usher in a socialist tyranny. This is one of the central themes of the infamous czarist-era forgery, *The Protocols of the Learned Elders of Zion,* the American publication of which Ford sponsored, and which is still widely reprinted and circulated as a virtual bible of anti-Semitism:

> We [the Jews] appear on the scene as alleged saviors of the worker from this oppression [of poverty] when we propose to him to enter the ranks of our fighting forces—Socialists, Anarchists, Communists—to whom we always give support in accordance with an alleged brotherly rule (of the solidarity of all humanity) of our social masonry. . . . By want and the envy and hatred which it engenders we shall move the mobs and with their hands we shall wipe out all those who hinder us on our way. . . . This hatred will be still further magnified by the effects of an economic crisis, which will stop dealing on the exchanges and bring industry to a standstill. We shall create by all the secret subterranean methods open to us and with the aid of gold, which is all in our hands, a universal economic crisis whereby we shall

throw upon the streets whole mobs of workers simultaneously in all the countries of Europe.

The survival of this fantasy into our own day can be seen in
such places as the 1991 book *The New World Order*, by the prominent leader of the so-called Christian Right, Pat Robertson. In its
pages, Robertson repeats such traditional anti-Semitic fare as
warnings about a conspiracy of "European bankers" and the sinister
dealings of various occult organizations supposedly financed by the
riches of the Rothschilds, whose ultimate goal is to foment worldwide revolution:

> That same year, 1792, the headquarters of Illuminated Free-
> masonry moved to Frankfurt, a center controlled by the Roth-
> schild family. It is reported that in Frankfurt, Jews for the first
> time were admitted to the order of Freemasons. If indeed
> members of the Rothschild family or their close associates
> were polluted by the occultism of Weishaupt's Illuminated
> Freemasonry, we may have discovered the link between the
> occult and the world of high finance. . . . New money sud-
> denly poured into the Frankfurt lodge, and from there a well-
> funded plan for world revolution was carried forth.

Then there's the image of Jews as cheapskates—selfish misers
who hoard every penny. No less a genius than Voltaire, the French
Enlightenment philosopher, wrote about the Jews throughout history as having been driven by greed. As historian Jerry Z. Muller

writes, Voltaire claimed that "Herod was unable to complete the re-building of the temple in Jerusalem because the Jews, though they loved their sanctuary, loved their money more."

In our own time, one vast underground river of ethnic humor that still flows steadily in many circles today is based on the suppos-edly well-known stinginess of Jews. In her book *In Cheap We Trust*, Lauren Weber quotes just a few samples:

> Why did the Jews wander in the desert for forty years? Be-cause one of them dropped a nickel.
> What's a Jewish dilemma? Free pork.
> And the truly vulgar: Have you heard the one about the Jewish pedophile? He's the guy who said, "Hey kids, go easy on the candy."

As Weber's interesting book points out, "Jews aren't the only ethnic group to have been branded with the scarlet letter C [for cheap]." Historically, ethnic stereotypes of stinginess have been ap-plied to the Scots, the Dutch, New Englanders, Scandinavians, Ger-mans, Japanese, and Chinese, among others. I would point out that the big difference is that the Jews are the only group to have also been branded with other interlinked stereotypes such as dishonesty, disloyalty, power-hunger, and a desire for world-domination. And, as a consequence, Jews alone have been the targets of pogroms and genocide. It's not nice for anyone to be considered cheap, but only for Jews can it be literally fatal.

Yet alongside this popular image of penny-pinching Jews there's a counter-image of Jews flaunting their wealth through inappropriate and vulgar displays—as in the 2006 movie *Keeping Up with the Steins,* featuring (according to the moviemakers) Benjamin Fiedler's "mega-bash," in which "the bar is more important than the mitzvah and a Jewish star means Neil Diamond," or the endless jokes about Jewish American Princesses. Silly and annoying? Of course, and also a reflection of deeper and more troubling currents of anti-Semitism even in some of America's seemingly most advanced academic settings. I'm thinking, for example, of the students at Cornell University who reportedly wore T-shirts reading SLAP-A-JAP! and BACK OFF BITCH, I'M A JAP-BUSTER!

Arch-capitalists—yet secret Communists. Ultra-cheap—yet flaunting their wealth. The apparently comfortable coexistence of these kinds of self-contradictions within the Jews-and-money stereotype helps make clear that belief in the stereotype isn't driven by logic but rather by the same dynamic that drives all anti-Semitism: hatred toward the "other" motivated by insecurity, ignorance, and fear.

And belief in the myths surrounding Jews and money is *certainly not* based on personal experience and observation of Jewish life and behavior. For even in a country like Japan, where the Jewish presence has always been minimal, anti-Semitic beliefs have become alarmingly popular. Essayist Daniel L. Alexander has described his personal encounters with these beliefs. In Alexander's words, "the

Japanese seem to have developed a horror and fascination with the Jews on a par with the strongest European traditions, and a surprising number of Japanese seem to enter political, economic, and intellectual life with Jews on the brain."

Alexander describes attending a lecture titled "The Jewish Mind and the Japanese Mind" delivered by a longtime Japanese resident, Jack Halpern, a former yeshiva student from Brooklyn and the son of Holocaust survivors who has made a career out of lecturing on the "international adaptability and business acumen" of the Jews— alleged traits many Japanese are apparently eager to emulate. But unfortunately, if predictably, the widespread sense of admiration for Jewish accomplishments co-exists with what Alexander calls "the nasty side of the Japanese fascination with Jews":

A coworker took me to a private estate for an exhibition of *netsuke,* the elaborately hand-carved traditional miniatures. Sipping tea in the rear garden, as the zithery sounds of a *koto* floated in the background, my coworker and I discussed the exhibition and the state of the art business with an organizer of the exhibition—who promptly blamed "that cabal of Jews who've bought up the stock market on the cheap" for the nation's economic strain then beginning to tell in sluggish fine-art sales.

In recent decades, a startlingly large number of popular books have been published in Japan that promote stereotypes about Jews and money. Some are directly based on *The Protocols of the Learned Elders of Zion*—for example, a 1973 best-seller titled *Nostradamus no daiyogen* (*The Great Prophecy of Nostradamus*) by Goto Ben and a similar 1986 book, *Yudaya ga wakaruto sekai ga mietekuru* (*To Watch Jews Is to See the World Clearly*) by Masami Uno. Uno, interestingly enough, believes that the Japanese are descendants of the legendary Lost Tribes of Israel, and he predicts that some day they will defeat the "fake Jews" who currently rule the world. Even mainstream political leaders have espoused Jewish conspiracy theories. Saito Eizaburo, a member of the House of Councillors (the Japanese equivalent of the United States Senate), authored a 1984 book titled *Sekai wo ugokasu yudaya pawag no himitsu* (*Secrets of the Jewish Power Which Controls the World*).

Experts on Japan have advanced various theories to explain the spread of anti-Semitic ideas in that country. Some focus on the on-going struggle of the Japanese to define their country's role in the modern world and the resulting array of conflicting values, attitudes, and desires that have arisen from that struggle. When people are having difficulty making sense of their place in a rapidly changing world, these analysts say, it's tempting to search for a scapegoat group to blame for their troubles. Others say that the Japanese attraction to *The Protocols*–style conspiracy theories about the Jews mirrors Japanese fascination with other similar fringe ideas, ranging from UFOs and ghosts to the occult. And still others point to the power of Western influences on Japanese culture, particularly through the influx of Christian missionaries and American military personnel in the post–World War II era, a portion of whom brought the infection of anti-Semitism to Japan. Some even point to the curious fact that, of all the plays of William Shakespeare, it was his anti-Semitic *Merchant of Venice* that was traditionally the most widely translated into Japanese. Millions of Japanese high school and college students were first exposed to the works of the world's greatest playwright—and to the image of the Jewish people— through the scurrilous character of Shylock.

But no matter the cause, the very existence of strong currents of anti-Semitism in Japan, so far from their origins in Christian Europe, underscores the seriousness of the challenge faced by well-meaning people who want to understand and then eliminate the crazy intellectual and psychological burden that stereotyped images of Jews impose on society.

We've seen some of the theological, historic, and economic roots to which the myths about Jews and money can be traced—and we've briefly glimpsed some of the weird forms those myths have taken in the minds of millions of people. What's the relationship between those myths and reality? Is there, in fact, anything unique and noteworthy about the relationship between the Jewish people and the world of money? I'll examine these questions in the next chapter.

3

THE FACTS
BEHIND
THE MYTHS

Anti-Semitism is not driven by reason. Like all forms of hatred, it is driven by the deepest wells of human emotion—fear, jealousy, insecurity, anxiety, resentment—and it is fundamentally not susceptible to logic. This is what makes it possible for anti-Semites to believe simultaneously in ideas that are mutually contradictory, with no apparent awareness of the incongruity; to believe things that obviously contradict their own experiences and personal observations; to selectively notice facts that seem to support their prejudices while ignoring others that might undermine them; and to return, over and over again, to stereotypes that are familiar and comfortable even after those images have been shown to be utterly divorced from reality. Bigotry appears to serve personal needs that are so profound—and so largely unconscious—that it is impervious to assault based purely on factual arguments.

The fact that anti-Semitism has no relation to logic is one reason why I generally refuse all invitations to "debate" purveyors of bigotry in public forums. (It certainly isn't because I worry that the arguments of my opponents would prove to be too formidable to rebut!) I know there is literally nothing I could say that would have any impact on the minds and hearts of those who are psychologically wedded to hatred.

And by agreeing to appear on the same stage or broadcast venue with an avowed anti-Semite, I would be lending a tinge of credibility and respectability to that person's position—as if admitting that there is a legitimate debate about anti-Semitism, with two sides that deserve a hearing. There's no actual controversy about intolerance, any more than there is a scientific debate about whether or not the moon is made of green cheese.

For this reason, it might seem superfluous for me to include in this book a chapter about the realities concerning Jews and money. "The people who believe the pernicious myths," one might say, "are not going to be convinced by the facts—and the rest of the world already knows the facts. So why waste your breath?"

Actually, I think the situation is not as black-and-white as this. It's true there are out-and-out bigots who will never change their attitudes no matter what an Abe Foxman might say. (In fact, I know from past experience that they are already writing their scathing attacks on this book to be posted online as "reviews" of its contents—long before the text is even available for reading!) But there are also millions of open-minded, well-intentioned people who, while not bigots, have been infected to a greater or lesser extent with some of the viruses of anti-Semitic beliefs.

These are people who may not have thought a lot about Jews or anti-Semitism but who have heard some of the myths that circulate in our society—in particular, myths about Jews and money—and have concluded that "Maybe there's some truth in what they say," or "I don't know many Jews, but I guess people wouldn't hate them without *some* good reason." The group includes many young people whose ideas about the world are still being formed by their schools, their peers, the media, and their own experiences, and who have not yet developed firm attitudes about racial, ethnic, and religious prejudices. And this sector of society also includes people who believe in their hearts that all bigotry and intolerance are wrong but may have been intimidated into silence or self-doubt by the loud voices of a few hateful individuals they may happen to know—in the workplace, in the community, or even in their own families.

This chapter is for all these people. Its purpose is to provide them with a sound, realistic perspective on the *real* relationship between Jews and money—to give them the facts that undermine the myths and make it easier to perceive the obvious realities that are everywhere in the world around us. I hope it will also provide some ammunition for people who may want to stand up to the bullies and bigots in their own environment but feel they lack the information to do so with confidence and authority.

As even a quick perusal of certain segments of the Internet will make clear, there's no shortage of disinformation about Jews and money to feed the attitudes of those who are determined to hate. In this chapter—as in my life's work—I am simply trying to do what I can to restore some balance.

With this goal in mind, let's consider some of the most common and widely believed myths about Jews and money, and the realities that belie them.

> Myth: Thanks to their innate abilities, their mutual loyalty, and their profound attachment to money, all Jews are wealthy.
> Reality: Like every community, Jews range from the very wealthy to the very poor.

Like virtually every population group in the United States, Jews came to this country as immigrants. And like most of these groups, the Jews have gradually worked their way from the bottom of the economic heap to more comfortable positions in the middle or even the top of the spectrum. It's a struggle that took decades of hard work on the part of millions of Jewish Americans, just as it did for the Irish Americans, the German Americans, the Italian Americans, and many other ethnic groups. Today we see millions of Hispanic Americans from many countries in Latin America as well as Asian Americans from countries such as Vietnam and Cambodia immersed in the same struggle—and with the same hope for eventual triumph.

Naturally, every American immigrant group has its unique characteristics. In the case of the Jews—particularly those who came to the United States from the 1880s into the 1930s—two special characteristics gave them an unusual economic and social status. On the one hand, many of them were fleeing from persecution: pogroms in Eastern Europe, discrimination in Western Europe, and ultimately the rise of genocidal anti-Semitism in Fascist Germany and Italy. This put them at an economic disadvantage as compared to some other immigrant groups. Whereas Christian immigrants from, say, Germany and Ireland could maintain close ties to friends, families, and communities in the homeland, even traveling back and forth as circumstances dictated, Jews who were fleeing oppression had no such luxury. They were thrown on their own resources in the New World, to sink or swim as fate dictated.

On the other hand, the flight from persecution also meant that the Jews who came to America included a larger-than-normal proportion of highly skilled, well-educated, professional people. A successful non-Jewish lawyer, professor, or doctor in a country like France or Italy was not very likely to emigrate to the United States, since he probably already enjoyed a comfortable existence at home. Those who did leave those countries were more likely to be poor laborers, the unskilled or the semi-skilled, who had to develop themselves intellectually and educationally in order to succeed in America.

But for Jews in Europe, persecution recognized no boundaries of education or status, and many of the Jews who fled to America were intellectually and professionally advanced. Naturally this gave them a relative advantage over their fellow immigrants when it came to competing for jobs and other sources of economic success.

The upshot of this mix of circumstances has been that, over the past two or three generations, Jews have become one of the more successful minority groups in the United States. We look with pride on our co-religionists who have achieved prominent places in American society—in business, law, medicine, education, politics, and other fields. And like many other ethnic groups, thousands of Jews have attained middle-class and upper-class status, together with the comforts and privileges that go with that status in contemporary American life. It's a classic story of the American dream, which everyone in this country can be gratified to recognize.

But though it is less gratifying to contemplate, it remains true that the image of the affluent and successful Jewish American is not the complete story of our life in this country. Like every subgroup in America, we have our pockets of poverty and suffering—people who have not been able to climb very high on the ladder of success, for whatever reasons.

The statistics tell part of the tale. Studies such as the National Jewish Population Survey, sponsored by United Jewish Communities and the Jewish federation system of charitable organizations, reveal that Jews in America suffer from poverty at a rate that is basically similar to that of other ethnic groups. As of the last survey, conducted in 2000–2001, approximately 7 percent of the American Jewish community live below the poverty line as defined by the federal government, but add to this number the Jewish people who live near the poverty line in homes considered "economically vulnerable" and the number jumps to 14 percent. This means that over 700,000 Jews in America fall into these categories, including 190,000 children.

Unfortunately, these numbers are likely to be underestimates, partly because so many poor Jews (like other people) are ashamed to admit their need, partly because many Jews live in urban centers where the cost of living is higher than average. This makes the income levels specified in the federal poverty guidelines less than adequate. For example, according to the 2010 guidelines, a family of four with an income of $22,050 is considered to be just above the poverty line. But if you've lived in a city such as New York, Los Angeles, or Miami—the three American cities with the largest concentrations of Jews—you know that this amount would scarcely provide a decent standard of living for four people.

For this reason, the authoritative Metropolitan Council on Jewish Poverty recommends using 150 percent of the federal poverty line as "a more realistic measure" in a city like New York. When this standard is adopted, we find that 20 percent of New York City's Jews—over 348,000 people—live at or below the poverty line.

Of course, specific subgroups within New York City's Jewish community suffer most from poverty. According to the same Metropolitan Council on Jewish Poverty:

> The Jewish poor are more likely to be married couples and live in neighborhoods with extensive Jewish infrastructure, including synagogues, day schools, kosher butchers, etc. The cost of living for them can be as much as 25% higher [than for non-Jews].
>
> The Jewish poor are often recent refugees from the former Soviet Union. Not just Russian Jews. But Jews from Uzbekistan, Turkmenistan, and Georgia. Many of these people are entirely new to Western ways, making their adjustment to life in America especially difficult.
>
> The Jewish poor also include Hasidic households in Brooklyn that have been blessed with many children, but lack the means to adequately clothe and feed their families.
>
> In Brooklyn, a substantial number of poor Jewish individuals are young adults and children. By contrast, in the Bronx, Manhattan and Queens, the Jewish poor are more likely to be senior citizens. Poor women still outnumber poor men by about 14%. A significant percentage of the needy are intact families with children. Fully 57% of New York's Jewish poor are married.

Perhaps most tragic, statistics compiled by the Holocaust Survivors Foundation suggest that about 25 percent of American survivors of the Holocaust are living in poverty (currently close to 30,000 people). It's sad to think that, after all they've lived through, these individuals are unable to enjoy a comfortable and secure old age in their adopted homeland.

Thankfully, more fortunate members of the Jewish community take their obligations to the Jewish poor very seriously. Countless charitable outreach programs have been created that do much to alleviate the worst suffering of poor Jewish families. In New York alone, the Metropolitan Council serves over 100,000 clients with services that include affordable housing initiatives, career services, crisis intervention and family violence services, health insurance enrollment assistance, home care programs, immigrant services, and kosher food distribution. On a national scale, the Jewish Federations of North America, representing 157 Jewish Federations and 400 Network communities, raise and distribute more than $3 billion annually for social welfare, social services, and educational needs, many of them targeted to the poor (both Jewish and non-Jewish).

Nonetheless, the reality of Jewish poverty is a sobering one. Anti-Semitic myths would suggest that Jews are a privileged elite in America. In fact, Jews are just another ethnic minority, with both winners and losers in the race for economic success. The same is true of Jews in other parts of the world—in Europe, Latin America, and Asia. It may make for a less dramatic story than the myth of Jewish privilege, but it's a reality.

Myth: Jews accumulate wealth by hoarding, an outgrowth
of their natural stinginess.

Reality: As a community, Jews appear to be among the most generous donors and philanthropists in American society.

The facts show that few if any ethnic or religious groups in America have created as large, powerful, and effective a force for charitable giving and work as American Jews. If Jewish Americans have been blessed with their fair share of economic good fortune—and they have—they have also repaid that bounty with exceptional generosity toward their fellow citizens.

Jewish philanthropy in the United States flows through several channels. The most traditional is the so-called federations—umbrella organizations comparable to the United Way that support thousands of charitable purposes throughout the country and around the world. All are united by what the Jewish Federations of North America describe as three core values: *tikkun olam* (repairing the world), *tzedakah* (charity and social justice) and *Torah* (Jewish learning). Taken together, the Jewish federation movement makes up one of the ten largest charitable organizations in the United States. Bear in mind that Jews constitute just under 2 percent of the total population of the country (approximately 5.1 million people out of a total population of over 300 million). Even so, Gary Tobin, an expert on philanthropy, estimated that federation donations make up only about 10 to 15 percent of the total funds raised by Jews for Jewish-related causes in the United States—so, as huge as the federation movement is, it's just a small part of the charitable giving by American Jews.

Private foundations created and supported by Jews constitute a second important stream of Jewish giving. Tobin estimated the number of these foundations at around 7,000, with total assets of $10 to $15 billion. If correct, that would make Jewish foundations almost 18 percent of the total 39,000 private foundations identified by the Foundation Center—another enormous disproportion in view of the tiny size of the Jewish population.

A third stream is donations to specifically Jewish religious, ethnic, and national institutions, including support for synagogues and temples, religious schools, and needy organizations in the state of Israel.

And a fourth stream—and by most accounts the fastest growing—is what researcher Gary Tobin called "the philanthropic mainstream," referring to a variety of institutions and organizations in the realms of education, health, human services, culture, politics, and others. Some of these organizations are oriented toward serving the Jewish community, but many are not. In fact, more and more Jewish giving is simply part of the vast flood of philanthropic generosity that millions of Americans participate in—a natural evolutionary step as Jews become more and more widely accepted in all facets of our national life.

It's difficult to pin down hard numbers about charitable giving by various ethnic or religious groups. Many donations by people of every ethnic background are anonymous or private. Millions of small gifts—$10, $100, $500 at a time—go unnoticed in the media and are scarcely identifiable by social group. But the numbers that are available, such as the statistics on foundations and the $3 billion raised annually by the Jewish Federations of North America alone, suggest that the Jewish community "swings above its weight" when it comes to philanthropic giving.

Another indication of the generosity of American Jews can be found by perusing lists such as the *Chronicle of Philanthropy*'s annual register of the largest charitable donations. The most recent list, covering sixty gifts made in 2009, includes a disproportionately large number of Jewish donors, from the largest gift of the year—the $705 million donated by Stanley and Fiona Druckenmiller to their family foundation, which supports medical research, education, and poverty-fighting efforts—down to number 56 on the list—$13.7 million given by Jeffrey Skoll, founding president of eBay, to the Skoll Foundation, which supports social entrepreneurship and venture capital in the Middle East, including the Palestinian territories. The whole list is dotted with well-known Jewish names: New York's Mayor Michael Bloomberg, financier George Soros, home builder Eli Broad, banker Sanford Weill, and several others.

The evidence seems clear: Jews may be 2 percent of the U.S. population, but they are responsible for a lot more than 2 percent of the charitable giving. It's a track record that doesn't exactly square with the anti-Semitic stereotype of the cheap, grasping Jew.

> Myth: Powerful Jews dominate and practically control the world of business.
>
> Reality: There are powerful Jews in business, but the vast majority of U.S. and world business leaders are non-Jewish.

We can easily imagine the anti-Semite who clings to stereotypes, when confronted with the evidence of Jewish generosity, fleeing to a new variation on the theme: "Of course Jews give flashy checks to charity! That's because they control the business world! They own the banks, the investment houses, and half the big corporations on the planet. No matter how much they give back, it's only a fraction of what they steal from the rest of us!"

The idea that Jews are prominent in business is one anti-Semitic myth that does have a glimmer of truth behind it. Jews have enjoyed success in the business world in numbers out of proportion to their share of the population. In the previous chapter, we discussed some of the reasons for this phenomenon—historical factors such as the long-term exclusion of Jews from occupations *other than* finance and trade, which drove many into becoming experts in those fields just as the emergence of modern capitalism was making them into some of the most lucrative and significant areas of endeavor.

We see a similar dynamic in many areas where discrimination and exclusion force a particular group into one or two pathways.

When African Americans were permitted to rise only in such fields as sports and entertainment, they focused much of their talent and ambition into those areas and soon came to dominate entire arenas, from professional football to popular music. Perhaps if Jews had been legally permitted only to be basketball players, they would rule today's NBA! (Don't laugh—back in the 1920s and 1930s, Jewish immigrants were among the leading hoops stars. One historian has commented, "Sportswriters then used to wax about the gaudy skills of 'natural athletes.' Sounds familiar, except the stars had names like Dutch Garfinkel and Doc Lou Sugerman, and the top teams were the Philadelphia 'Hebrews,' the New York Whirlwinds and the Cleveland Rosenblums." That's the way societal pressures impact people.)

Furthermore, in fields like finance, where European Jews developed traditions and skills that they later imported to America, the prominence of Jews in the industry may be slightly exaggerated by the ubiquity of Jewish *names* in company logos. Why? Again, exclusionary practices played a part. Until the 1970s, most of the great banking and investment companies on Wall Street wouldn't hire a Jewish associate, no matter how talented and brilliant. In defense, the Jews started their own firms, which soon competed on an equal footing against those that hired gentiles. As a result, companies like Goldman Sachs, Kuhn Loeb, Oppenheimer & Company, Lehman Brothers, and Lazard Frères rose to international prominence—and the family names above the doors soon attracted attention, including scowls from anti-Semites whenever anything controversial happened in the world of high finance.

We're still seeing those scowls today, often in a rather subtle form. Consider this passage from a summer 2009 article about Goldman Sachs by talented journalist Matt Taibbi: "The world's most powerful investment bank is a great vampire squid wrapped around the face of humanity, relentlessly jamming its blood funnel into anything that smells like money."

I don't know if Matt Taibbi is anti-Semitic or even whether he harbors anti-Semitic ideas. Clearly, he feels strongly about the dangers of financial market manipulation, and in that he is right. But Taibbi's image of the Jewish-owned investment bank as a "vampire squid" flirts dangerously with vicious old stereotypes. As journalist Michael Kinsley later wrote, "This sentence, many have charged, goes beyond stereotypes about Jews and money, touches other classic anti-Semitic themes about Jews as foreign or inhuman elements poisoning humanity and society, and—to some critics—even seems to reference the notorious 'blood libel' that Jews use the blood of Christian babies to make matzoh." Historians of anti-Semitism point out that the image of the Jew as vampire was a common one in bigoted writings of the nineteenth and early twentieth centuries.

I think Kinsley's comments about the article by Taibbi get it just about right. Noting that Taibbi has vigorously denied any connection between his "vampire squid" image and the classic anti-Semitic stereotype (and has called the idea that his article might have been anti-Semitic "ludicrous"), Kinsley expresses puzzlement. He wonders, "Could such a sophisticated writer (the article skewers Goldman with great skill and style) actually not know about the stereotypes and ancient lies that this passage echoes, and could he actually be surprised that there would be people calling his article, fairly or otherwise, anti-semitic?" I find myself wondering the same thing.

Again, let me stress—I don't want to accuse Matt Taibbi of being anti-Semitic. It's very possible that his use of the age-old "vampire" slur was inadvertent and coincidental. This is a perfect illustration of the dangers posed by the strong foothold that ancient anti-Semitic ideas have in our collective unconscious. They lie around in wait, ready to be activated when a writer like Taibbi, deliberately or not, evokes them—and with them, the fear, mistrust, and hatred they carry.

Of course, no one thinks about or even notices the religious affiliations of the founders of such large, wealthy, and powerful financial institutions as Morgan Stanley, Bank of America, Barclays, Credit Suisse, or Nomura. But again, the person infected with prejudice will tend to notice details that support his worldview and simply ignore others that contradict it—so the Jewish-sounding names stand out on any list of bankers while the others simply fade into the background.

Much the same is true in other fields of business. Take Hollywood and the media in general, where one of the stock claims by anti-Semites is that Jews control the industry and manipulate it to the benefit of "their people." Actually, when it comes to entertainment, the idea that Jews are unusually successful does have a grain of truth. In about three seconds on Google you can find a list of prominent Jews in the American media, and it's quite impressive—from Sumner Redstone and Michael Eisner to Steven Spielberg and Larry King. There's no denying Jews have made their mark in Hollywood.

On the other hand, it's not hard to name non-Jews with equally prominent roles in the world of media. You can match Sumner Redstone up with Rupert Murdoch; Michael Eisner with Tom Hanks; Steven Spielberg with James Cameron; Larry King with Oprah Winfrey.

Yes, I'm joking—in a way. If "Name the Jew" versus "Name the gentile" seems like a silly game, that's because it is. The fact is that for all their prominence in Hollywood, Jews do not control the entertainment industry—not as individuals, and certainly not as Jews. How many movies with overtly Jewish themes get produced in a typical year? No more than a handful. The last major example that springs to mind is the 2009 film *Inglourious Basterds*—and that was the brainchild of Quentin Tarantino (who, for the record, was born in Knoxville of parents with Irish, Italian, and Cherokee heritage, and has been quoted as saying, "Movies are my religion"). So much for Jewish control of the media.

When you turn to other major industries, from oil to agribusiness to computers to automaking, you quickly discover that the Jewish names in the executive offices are few and far between. Anti-Semites love to claim that Jews control most of the world's wealth—but the last time I looked, neither Warren Buffett nor Bill Gates was Jewish.

When it comes to maintaining belief in a cherished myth, a few selective perceptions can go a long, long way.

> Myth: Jewish religious teachings and culture emphasize the value of wealth and condone its accumulation by any means necessary.
>
> Reality: Ethical concern for one's fellow human beings, including charity, generosity, and justice, are at the core of Jewish religion and tradition.

As we've seen, anti-Semitic thinking holds that Jews have a special affinity for money. For Karl Marx, this meant that money was, in effect, the true God of the Jew, the moral center around which his universe revolved. Countless other thinkers have echoed this stereotype through the ages. To cite just one example, the German economic historian Werner Sombart (1863–1941), in his book *The Jews and Modern Capitalism,* approvingly quoted the "contemporary opinion" that "These people [the Jews] have no other God but the unrighteous

Mammon, and no other aim than to get possession of Christian property." He went on to say, "Let me avow it right away: I think that the Jewish religion has the same leading ideas as Capitalism. I see the same spirit in the one as in the other." Sombart was at pains to search out passages from the Hebrew scriptures that supposedly demonstrated this affinity—for example, Deuteronomy 15:6, which reads, "For the Lord, thy God, will bless thee, as He promised thee; and thou shalt lend unto many nations, but thou shalt not borrow."

It doesn't require much immersion in Jewish culture, however, to recognize what a bizarrely inaccurate stereotype this is. If anything, Jewish religion and tradition are exceptional on the world stage for the special emphasis they give to generosity, charity, and fair economic dealings with one's fellow human beings. And to demonstrate this requires not the fine-tooth comb that Sombart used to identify Bible passages that praised the value of wealth. One can point to countless quotations from the great Jewish teachers of every era that stress these themes.

Here are just a handful of examples:

- According to the Talmud, the collection of Jewish law and tradition dating from the fifth and sixth centuries, the *first* question we'll be asked when we are brought before the heavenly court for judgment is, "Did you conduct your business affairs honestly?" (*Shabbat* 31a).

- The sage Rabbi Yossi, in the compilation *Ethics of the Fathers,* offers the following guideline about moral business dealings: "Let your fellow's money be as precious to you as your own" (*Ethics* 2:7).

- The Talmud makes it clear that charity is not optional but mandatory, even for a poor person: "If a man sees that his livelihood is barely sufficient for him, he should give charity from it" (*Gittin* 7a).

- The Torah reminds us of the importance of charity again and again: "For there will never cease to be needy people in your land, which is why I command you: open your hand to the poor and needy" (Deuteronomy 15:11).

- Jewish tradition even equates giving charity with honoring God himself. Thus the Talmud declares, "If a person closes his eyes to avoid giving charity, it is as if he committed idolatry." And Rabbi Adin Steinsaltz, a popular modern commentator, explains this: "A person who knows that his money comes from God will give from his money to the poor. One who does not give to the poor, however, apparently believes that his own strength and wisdom are solely responsible for all he has. This is a form of idolatry." Thus, only the charitable person can claim to truly honor God.

Do these sound like the teachings of a people for whom the accumulation of wealth is the greatest good?

What's more, Judaism has also been blessed with some unique traditions that center on the importance of generosity and charity in managing one's money. One of these is tithing—the giving of a fixed percentage of one's income to charitable purposes, which was treated in many self-governing Jewish communities in medieval times not merely as an admirable custom but as a legal requirement. Another was the tradition of *Shmita*, or the sabbatical year, during which lands were to remain fallow, in part as a way of revitalizing agricultural productivity. But the tradition also required that, at the end of the Shmita year, personal debts would be nullified and forgiven. Similarly, the tradition of the Jubilee year held that every 49 years all property would be returned to its original owners and any indentured servant would be given his freedom. Both the Shmita and Jubilee traditions were designed to minimize the opportunities for individuals to accumulate excessive wealth, while giving those of lesser status a chance to improve their condition.

Christians also have their traditions of charitable giving and compassion for the less fortunate, of which they are justly proud. But these Christian values were inherited directly from their "elder siblings," the Jews, who placed justice and charity at the very center of their ethical and religious teachings. The notion that Judaism in any way sanctions acquisitiveness or greed is a preposterous fiction that wouldn't exist if not for anti-Semitism.

> Myth: Jewish tradition holds that it is acceptable to exploit and even cheat non-Jews.
> Reality: Jewish teachings emphasize the importance of fair dealing and justice toward all people, Jews and non-Jews alike.

One persistent element of the stereotyped notions about Jews and money is the idea that Jews—the "chosen people"—believe they have a special relationship with God that privileges them to harm other people with impunity. It's a canard that can be traced back at least as far as the writings of Martin Luther (1483–1546), one of the founders of the Protestant Reformation. In his anti-Semitic text, *On the Jews and Their Lies,* Luther wrote:

> [T]heir Talmud and their rabbis record that it is no sin for a Jew to kill a Gentile, but it is only a sin for him to kill a brother Israelite. Nor is it a sin for a Jew to break his oath to a Gentile. Likewise, they say that it is rendering God a service to steal or rob from a Goy, as they in fact do through their usury. For since they believe that they are the noble blood and the circumcised saints and we the accursed Goyim, they cannot treat us too harshly or commit sin against us, for they are the lords of the world and we are their servants, yes their cattle. . . .

There's a psychological phenomenon known as projection, in which a person unconsciously denies his own attributes and instead ascribes them to other people. It's not difficult to see projection at work in this accusation. Consider the historical facts. In medieval and Renaissance Europe, Jews were systematically singled out by civil and religious authorities for opprobrium, forbidden to live and work as they liked, subject to special confiscatory taxes, and periodically plundered of their property by the Inquisition or in pogroms. Jews, of course, did none of these things to Christians (and would have been powerless to do so had they wished to). But in this passage by Luther, we have an important Christian theologian accusing the Jews of considering it moral to mistreat another group of people solely on account of their religious difference! If it's possible for a psychological mechanism like projection to operate among a large community of people, this accusation clearly represents the strange effect that a guilty conscience can have on minds that find it intolerable to acknowledge their own sinfulness.

As for the truth behind this myth, here again the teachings of Jewish tradition are very clear: Jews are expected to show charity, compassion, and honesty toward all people, both Jewish and gentile, not only in financial matters but in all areas of behavior. Any insinuation to the contrary is a simple libel against the honor of the Jewish people.

For example, consider this admonition from the Babylonian Talmud: "We must provide help for the non-Jewish poor as well as for the Jewish poor; we must visit non-Jews when they are sick as well as our fellow Jews when they are sick; and we must attend to the burial of their dead as well as the burial of our own dead; for these are the ways of peace" (*Gittin* 61a).

Nor are the traditional admonitions to Jews to be generous to non-Jews merely empty words. They are actually the basis of Jewish behavior in the real world. As Gary Tobin said in the article on Jewish philanthropy cited earlier,

> *Tzedakah* is also dedicated to serving the world-at-large, non-Jews as well as Jews. The need to "repair a broken world" [*tikkun olam*] is deeply embedded in community values and norms. A strong universalistic component characterizes Jewish philanthropy. The interest in social justice and volunteering evolves constantly. It continues to take new forms, such as the Jewish Service Corps, which is designed to serve the secular rather than the Jewish world.

Tobin noted that although Jewish philanthropists contribute substantially to Jewish causes on an annual basis, they tend to make megagifts of $10 million to $50 million or more to non-Jewish philanthropies over a five- or ten-year period of time. He found "evidence that Jewish philanthropists are more likely to make their largest gifts to non-Jewish philanthropies" and that "it is less common to see megagifts given to the Jewish community. Universities, symphonies, hospitals, and museums are capturing the largest gifts from Jewish donors."

Far from restricting their giving solely to Jewish institutions or causes, Jewish donors actually make a special effort to spread the benefits of their generosity as widely through society as possible—a clear contradiction of the anti-Semitic stereotype.

> Myth: Jews use their power and influence to benefit "their own kind."
>
> Reality: Jews are like most other Americans—public-spirited, patriotic, and with widely varying political and social agendas.

Anti-Semites sometimes like to blend two of the pillars of their mistaken beliefs—the accusation of disloyalty and the stereotyped connection between Jews and money—into a hybrid belief that Jews use their (highly exaggerated) wealth and power not to benefit America or humanity in general but to advance their own secret agenda—mainly, to amass still more wealth and power in Jewish hands.

This would be a potent accusation if true. The problem is that so much evidence undermines it. For example, we've already looked at the fact that Jewish Americans make ample and generous charitable contributions to non-Jewish causes. Examine the donor rolls of hospitals, universities, museums, and social programs in cities and towns throughout the United States. The chances are quite good that local Jewish Americans along with many other community residents have played a big role in supporting these institutions and programs for the good of all.

Consider another arena. If Jews were universally self-interested in accumulating wealth, wouldn't you expect them to use their political influence on behalf of parties and candidates that promote capitalist causes and boost the rich at the expense of ordinary people? That would seem to be logical, but it's the opposite of how most Jewish Americans have actually voted. To the chagrin of some conservatives, the American Jewish community has always been unusually liberal in its political habits, including donations to candidates and, as best as polls and surveys can determine, in its voting patterns. Jewish liberalism is the basis of the community's longstanding historic alliance with African Americans in support of civil rights. Notable among the founders of the National Association for the Advancement of Colored People were Julius Rosenwald and Henry Moscowitz.

As the scholar and wit Milton Himmelfarb famously said, "Jews earn like Episcopalians and vote like Puerto Ricans." It may not have been a politically correct way of phrasing it, but the observation was fundamentally accurate.

This is not to say that Jews are monolithic, either in their politics or in any other way. Today there are quite a few prominent Jewish voices on the conservative side of the spectrum, from Nobel Prize–winning economist Milton Friedman to the libertarian former chairman of the Federal Reserve Alan Greenspan. Is there a clear pattern here? Not particularly.

This brings us to the only logical conclusion we can draw about the Jews after having examined each of these anti-Semitic myths and found them wanting. In the end, Jews are merely people, with the same widely varying characteristics, beliefs, attitudes, and behaviors that all people have. I personally think the Jews of America have done much good that they can be proud of, but then I'm biased in their favor! And the truth is that much the same could be said of every other ethnic or religious group that is part of our nation's tapestry.

The point is not that all Jews are angels—of course they're not, any more than all the members of any other group are perfect. The point is that the vicious stereotypes that bigots and thoughtless people have attached to the Jews are no more grounded in reality than the hateful stereotypes historically attached to any other ethnic, religious, or national group—and this lack of reality applies especially to the phony beliefs about Jews and money that the bigots continue to promote.

The best antidote for all those canards is a very simple one—the truth.

4
THE
STEREOTYPE
TODAY

Some of the most blatant forms of the Jews-and-money stereotype have now faded away in the light of reality, especially among the more enlightened segments of society—for which we are thankful. The stereotype, nonetheless, is surprisingly and stubbornly persistent—despite the wide gulf between it and the realities of Jewish history and contemporary life.

How do we know this? Is there any way to actually measure the degree to which people in the United States and around the world subscribe to biased beliefs about Jews?

Actually, there is. The Anti-Defamation League has for years conducted periodic surveys scientifically designed to measure the existence of anti-Semitic propensities in representative samples of people. The most recent U.S. survey, conducted by telephone in September and October of 2009, included 1,747 adults, with an oversampling of African Americans and Hispanics that was designed to increase the reliability of our findings in regard to those two subgroups. The results, while subject to the same risk of uncertainty or error as any other professionally designed survey, should be accurate to within a margin of error of plus or minus 4 percent.

This latest survey contains both good news and not-so-good news. The good news: Anti-Semitic propensities as measured by responses to an eleven-item anti-Semitic Index developed by ADL in 1964 are now at a historic low, matching the previous low point in 1998. Those who agree with six or more of the eleven prejudicial statements in the index are considered to have anti-Semitic propensities. In 2009, according to the index, 12 percent of Americans had anti-Semitic propensities, down from 15 percent in 2007, 17 percent in 2002, and 29 percent back in 1964. This is undeniably good news, and we at ADL celebrate it—as all Americans should.

The bad news—or at least the not-so-good news—is that anti-Semitic ideas still have a significant foothold among portions of the U.S. citizenry. And these include several ideas that form part of what we're calling the Jews-and-money stereotype.

According to the survey findings:

- Eighteen percent of Americans agree that it's probably true that "Jews have too much power in the business world."
- Fifteen percent agree that "Jews have too much control and influence on Wall Street."
- Thirteen percent agree that "Jews have too much power in the U.S. today."
- Thirteen percent agree that "Jews are more willing than others to use shady practices to get what they want."
- Thirteen percent agree that "Jewish business people are so shrewd that others don't have a fair chance at competition."

- Twelve percent agree that "Jews are not just as honest as other businesspeople."

Fortunately, these percentages are relatively low and falling. But they represent enormous absolute numbers. Twelve percent of the U.S. population represents some 37 million people—and that's just those who are willing to *admit* to a pollster that they harbor anti-Semitic beliefs.

Certain subgroups of the population reveal patterns that are also disturbing. Those with lower levels of education are more likely to hold anti-Semitic views—for example, fully 19.5 percent of respondents without college backgrounds agreed with six or more of the eleven survey statements. Those who rank overall among the most anti-Semitic are extremely likely to agree with the statements regarding excessive Jewish power in American society—for instance, 79 percent of those with anti-Semitic propensities agree that Jews wield "too much power in business." And anti-Semitic propensities among African Americans, while declining, are significantly higher than among the general population—28 percent in 2009, as compared to 12 percent among all Americans.

The ADL periodically commissions similar studies in Europe. The last such survey, conducted between December 2008 and January 2009, examined attitudes among citizens of seven European nations—Austria, France, Hungary, Poland, Germany, Spain, and the

United Kingdom. A total of 3,500 individuals were surveyed, and the same margin of error of plus or minus 4 percent was obtained for each country's results.

For this survey, five statements were rated by respondents, two of which related to the Jews-and-money stereotype: "Jews have too much power in the business world" and "Jews have too much power in international financial markets." A disturbingly high percentage of the Europeans surveyed expressed agreement with these beliefs. For example, 40 percent of those surveyed agreed that Jews have "too much power in the business world," with particularly high levels of agreement in certain countries (Poland, 55 percent; Spain, 56 percent; Hungary, 67 percent). Forty-one percent agreed that Jews have "too much power in international financial markets," with the same three countries rising to the top of the list (Poland, 54 percent; Hungary, 59 percent; Spain, 74 percent). Almost one-third—32 percent—of those surveyed believed that at least three of the five statements about Jews were "probably true," a percentage that has remained about the same since the previous survey (taken in 2007).

Perhaps most troubling, in the 2009 survey—taken during the height of the global economic crisis—31 percent of the Europeans surveyed said Jews were to blame at least in part for the crisis.

What accounts for the disturbing persistence of stereotyped beliefs about Jews? Sociologists, historians, psychologists, and political scientists have advanced a variety of theories. For me, the most basic reason is that bigotry and hatred are powerful political and psychological tools. For weak or unscrupulous people, they serve as emotional crutches, giving them the license to blame "the other" for their own inadequacies or failures; for those seeking power, they can be used to stir up strong reactions in the crowd, attract attention, and galvanize people into action.

For those with a political ax to grind, stereotyping is a particularly useful weapon. For example, the Jews-and-money stereotype is extraordinarily popular among anti-Israel groups in the Middle East. They use it not only to defend their own flirtation with, or outright embrace of, anti-Semitism, but also to claim that Israel's survival reflects not its moral status as a nation among nations but rather the manipulation of world opinion and, especially, of U.S. policy by wealthy, self-interested Jews.

Many people don't realize that classic anti-Semitism is a relatively recent phenomenon in the Muslim world.

As we noted in chapter 2, Jews played a significant role in the culture and economies of Muslim countries during the Middle Ages

---

* Just to dispose of a semantic objection that is often raised: Yes, Muslims can be anti-Semitic, even though the Arabs are themselves a Semitic race. The word "anti-Semitism" is used by me and by the vast majority of observers to mean "bigoted hatred directed against Jews and Judaism," not literally "hatred of Semites." So, of course, a Muslim—even an Arab one—can be an anti-Semite.

and Renaissance, countries in which they were often treated with greater tolerance and respect than in Christian Europe. Not until the nineteenth century did European-style anti-Semitism, with its three deadly pillars—the accusation of deicide, the imputation of disloyalty, and its stereotypes regarding Jews and money—begin to spread throughout the Islamic world.

Today, traditional anti-Semitism is rampant in many Muslim countries. It is exacerbated by tensions over the ongoing conflict in the Middle East, where the existence of the Jewish state of Israel in territory that many Arabs believe should be in Muslim hands is widely regarded as a cultural, political, and religious humiliation that must be avenged. It is also encouraged by governments in the region that are eager to use the specter of an outside enemy as a convenient scapegoat to distract attention from their own failures to create vibrant modern economies and to offer democratic freedoms to their peoples.

Thus we see, in one autocratic Middle East regime after another, government broadcasting and print media deliberately inflaming anti-Semitic hatred by publishing scurrilous news stories, hate-filled editorials and opinion columns, and vicious cartoons that repeat and embellish all the traditional anti-Jewish canards—including, of course, the stereotypes regarding Jews and money.

The same anti-Semitic tropes that appear in such blatant forms in the Muslim media also crop up in non-Muslim countries. Cartoonist Khalil Bendib, who was born in France and raised mainly in

Morocco, now lives in Berkeley, California, and distributes his work through various, mostly Web-based, alternative media outlets. He takes a strongly pro-Palestinian position on the Middle East conflict, which is his right—but at times his imagery draws straight from the old cesspool of anti-Semitic stereotypes, which puts his work beyond the pale of respectability. I am thinking, for example, of a Bendib cartoon from 2001 depicting then-President George W. Bush holding a giant meat cleaver to the neck of a helpless Palestinian child, prone on a crude altar. Overhead we see a wrathful "god" carrying a giant moneybag labeled with the names of various Jewish and pro-Israeli organizations (including the ADL), and shouting orders to Bush. The caption reads, "And the Almighty Dollar said, 'Sacrifice me a Muslim son, or else!'" This image of an imaginary bloodthirsty Jewish cabal using its wealth to force the sacrificial slaughter of an innocent is classic, ugly anti-Semitism at its worst.

There's no question that the use of mass media to spread and reinforce anti-Semitic stereotypes has helped to poison the climate in which the peoples of the Middle East must live together. In her article "Observations: How Suicide Bombers Are Made," Italian journalist Fiamma Nirenstein writes, "Wherever one looks, from Cairo and Gaza to Damascus and Baghdad, from political and religious figures to writers and educators, from lawyers to pop stars, and in every organ of the media, the very people with whom the state of Israel is expected to live in peace have devoted themselves with ever greater ingenuity to slandering and demonizing the Jewish state, the Jewish people, and Judaism itself—and calling openly for their annihilation." Nirenstein goes on to observe:

> The Arab press has also helped itself to the rich trove of classical European anti-Semitism. Outstanding in this regard has been *Al-Abram,* Egypt's leading government-sponsored daily. One recent series related in great detail how Jews use the blood of Gentiles to make matzah for Passover. Not to be outdone, columnist Mustafa Mahmud informed his readers that, to understand the true intentions of the Jews, one must consult *The Protocols of the Elders of Zion,* in which the leaders of the international Jewish conspiracy acknowledge openly their "limitless ambitions, inexhaustible greed, merciless vengeance, and hatred beyond imagination. . . . Cunning," it allegedly declares, "is our approach, mystery is our way."

Even seemingly respectable Islamic theologians have gotten caught up in the impulse to hate the Jews and blame the ills of the world upon them. For example, in a 1968 conference at the University of Cairo sponsored by the Al-Azar Academy of Islamic Research, one well-known imam, professor, and mufti after another rose to attack Jews, Judaism, and Zionism, repeating, among other slurs, the stereotypes about Jews and money that so many others have embraced over the centuries. A few excerpts from the conference proceedings will suffice to convey the tone:

Evil, wickedness, breach of vows, and money-worship are inherent qualities in them [the Jews]. Many a time they were punished for their evil, but they never repented or gave up their sinfulness. They have usurped Palestine from its right owners, doing evil, shedding blood, ripping up pregnant women, blowing up villages, and disregarding and defying world opinion. . . .

They always try to seize any opportunity to take revenge on Islam and Muslims. . . .

The Jews harmed the Muslims economically [in Muhammad's time], because they had possessed most of the wealth in Medina and thus controlled the economic position. They used to adopt the same policy at all times. They dealt with loans, usury, and monopolized foods. They are characterized by avarice and many other vices, which arose from selfishness, love of worldly life, and envy. The Jews colluded with every hostile movement against the Islamic Call [to conversion] and the Muslims.

In the decades since that conference, far too many Muslim religious and secular leaders have continued to use similar rhetoric. Even more harmfully, these same beliefs are being passed on to future generations of Muslims through history textbooks, school curricula, and children's books.

The Islamic world isn't the only place where anti-Semitic beliefs play a useful political role. They are also popular among various groups in Western democracies, including both Europe and the United States. Among far-right, ultranationalist, anti-immigrant, and neofascist political organizations in Germany, France, and other European countries, anti-Semitism is part of a deadly cocktail of beliefs that are used to foster an us-versus-them mentality and to attract electoral support among the socially, psychologically, and economically insecure. If you can convince someone who is unemployed, financially struggling, or simply feeling alienated from a society that is changing rapidly around him that all his troubles are caused by a sinister other that has infiltrated his world, it's an easy next step to convince him to vote for a candidate who proposes to take stern measures to combat the threat.

Both before and since the fall of the Soviet Union, anti-Semitism has also been popular among nationalist groups in Russia. It has found its way periodically into official government propaganda, in which the Jews serve the role of scapegoats for societal ills that the authorities are unable or unwilling to remedy. Historian Ruth Okuneva compiled a collection of excerpts from Russian propaganda publications of the 1980s in which many of the traditional themes of anti-Semitism were evoked—including the stereotypes about Jews and money:

> The chief strategic aim of the Zionist movement is the establishment of its domination of the world. . . . Their obsession with the idea of world domination is the primary cause of the crimes which humanity has witnessed. . . . "God's chosen people" have their own laws, their own

sphere, their own destiny, whereas the despised *goyim* are suited only to be "tools with the power of speech," slaves. . . . The teachings of Judaism are pervaded with hatred for work and contempt for the man who spends his day in toil. The entire ideology of Judaism is not imbued with the idea of work, but with a narrow practicality, the means for making a profit, a mania for silver, the spirit of egoism, and the craving for money. . . . The Talmud teaches that one is forbidden to steal only from a *khaver* (a fellow-Jew). One is permitted to take everything from anyone else (the *goyim*), because God has reserved all non-Jewish wealth for the Jews.

In Russia and elsewhere in the former communist bloc, anti-Semitism motivated by political ideology blends inextricably with cultural and religious strands of anti-Semitism, some of them very ancient. The result is a culture in which anti-Jewish feeling is so deeply ingrained that it must feel profoundly normal to the people who grow up surrounded by it—so much so that its potentially deadly effects are practically invisible to them.

For example, whenever I visit Poland, I'm startled and dismayed to see wood carvings on the shelves of souvenir shops that are nothing more than anti-Semitic caricatures—images of bearded, long-nosed, black-hatted Jews, some wearing traditional prayer shawls, and all clutching bags or boxes containing piles of gold or counting coins with their fingers. When I ask about the meaning of these tasteless images, the shop owners are surprised at the question.

"They are good-luck tokens," they explain, "to be given to someone who has bought a new home or started a new job. The idea is to wish them the success and riches that the Jew enjoys!" The fact that I find these *tchotchkes* terribly inappropriate seems unfathomable to them.

And not only to the shop owners. When I've mentioned my dismay to Polish government officials and suggested that a national program of education about the dangers of stereotyping might be necessary, I've received only shrugs in response. The assumption seems to be that anti-Semitic stereotyping doesn't hurt anybody. This is a sadly blinkered attitude on the part of national leaders of a country in which citizen collaboration with the Nazi Holocaust during World War II was shockingly widespread, leading to the deaths of thousands of Jews. Stereotyping, harmless? Not really.

The deliberate use of anti-Semitism as a tool for political rabble-rousing can be seen at work among bigots of both far-right and far-left persuasions, both here in the United States and around the world.

We've already alluded to the persistence of old anti-Semitic slurs—including money-related slurs—among some in the so-called Christian right, such as Christian Coalition founder Pat Robertson. Swing a little further toward the fringe and you find the same ideas in even less veiled form among many far-right hate groups, such as those in the newly resurgent militia movement.

The Turner Diaries, a classic hate manual in novel form written by William L. Pierce (under the pseudonym of Andrew Macdonald) that has sold more than a quarter of a million copies since its first publication in 1978, paints a graphic picture of a violent white rebellion against the tyranny of liberals, nonwhites, and Jews. A popular read among neo-Nazi groups such as The Order, it is believed to have been one of the inspirations for Timothy McVeigh's bombing of the Federal Building in Oklahoma City in 1995.

In his book *The Racist Mind,* psychologist Raphael S. Ezekiel described his extensive conversations with white racists, including members of the Ku Klux Klan and other hate groups, in an attempt to delve into the attitudes and motivations that shape their bigotry. The book includes a memorable, chilling description of his attendance at a meeting of the Aryan Nations organization, in which the age-old myths about Jews and money were deployed as part of an array of propaganda designed to stir up anti-Semitic hatred:

> [T]he altar is dominated by an upright Roman sword, the symbol of the organization and its version of the Cross. This sword, this Cross, bears a swastika at its hilt. A memorial wreath to Rudolf Hess, Hitler's lieutenant who had died not long before, stands beside the altar.
>
> The speeches begin and run through the day. . . .
>
> The first speaker . . . complains about the use of condoms [and] attacks what he calls "AIDS groups." The second speaker, a retired military officer [declares that] since

the Russian Revolution, 140 million people had been slain "by the Jew Talmudic Communists."

Every evil, he tells us, comes from money. "And behind money is the Zionist Talmudic Jew." The Federal Reserve System, he tells us, is a private system owned by eight banks, all of them Jewish, four of them foreign; his list includes Warburg, Lazard Frères, Rothschild, Kuhn-Loeb, and Chase Manhattan. We must get rid of the Federal Reserve System and of the income tax. We must repudiate the national debt.

"We must," he goes on, "tell the people at the top: There will be treason trials! You will be strung from the trees!"

The room explodes in loud applause. Cries of "*Hail Victory!*" [English for the Nazi shout, *Sieg Heil.*] Cries of "*White Power!*"

Similar beliefs are prominent in the weird and outrageous political mythology of the almost unclassifiable Lyndon LaRouche. A political opportunist whose affiliations have ranged wildly over the past three decades from various avowedly socialist groups to the Democratic party as a candidate in several primaries and then to a series of independent parties, LaRouche's political views are a mélange of conspiracy theories that mash together supposed threats from communists, international drug dealers, the FBI, the CIA, agents of Libya, the Council on Foreign Relations, the British royal family, and a number of long-time staples of right-wing fear-mongering, such as "global bankers." And a running thread in all of LaRouche's ideological ramblings is the belief that Jews form a secret global cartel that manipulates governments for their own bene-fit and to the detriment of all others.

A few years ago, it appeared that LaRouchism had run its course. Unfortunately, there are signs that LaRouche and his ideas have achieved some new traction since the financial meltdown of 2008–2009. LaRouche has gained prestige and even a reputation as a savant in some circles by claiming to have "predicted" the economic crisis. Of course, if you spin out fanciful theories about future events for decades, including frequent prophecies of imminent disaster, eventually one of these prophecies is likely to appear prescient—and that is just what happened to LaRouche.

Nonetheless, LaRouche has been praised by, for example, the Italian newspaper *Corriere della Sera* as "the guru politician who, since the nineties, has announced the crash of speculative finances and the need for a new Bretton Woods," and Italian Euro-parliamen-tarian Mario Borghezio of the Northern League has been quoted as calling LaRouche, "an heretical economist who had forecast the fi-nancial crisis much in advance, and who has long since developed a lucid and deep analysis of the distortions in the world economic sys-tem." It's disturbing to see such respect accorded a crackpot whose ideas have scarcely mellowed over the years. Just last year LaRouche inserted himself into the debate over health care reform with a com-parison of President Obama to Adolf Hitler, and the warning that Americans must "quickly and suddenly change the behavior of this president . . . for no lesser reason than that your sister might not end up in somebody's gas oven."

The far right, unfortunately, doesn't have a monopoly on the exploitation of anti-Jewish sentiment. As I wrote in my book *Never Again?*, the ongoing conflict in the Middle East has created a new opportunity for peddlers of anti-Semitism to gain a foothold among those who historically rejected it:

> Those who consider themselves "liberal" or "left-wing" around the world, including both Europe and the United States, often lean toward the Palestinian side in the [Middle East] conflict. They do so because of their traditional antipathy to imperialism as practiced by the great Western powers, including the United States, Britain, and France. This leads them to favor what they perceive as the "Third World" side in any international dispute. In this case, that means the Palestinians, who are indeed a poor, dispossessed people deserving of sympathy (and of far better treatment than they've ever received at the hands of the Jordanians and other Arab nationalities that publicly espouse their cause).
>
> Most of these liberal sympathizers with the Palestinian cause denounce the terrorism practiced by some Islamic extremists (although a few excuse it). But the liberals seem to reserve their harshest criticism for Israeli policies. Many overlook or rationalize the use of violence by Palestinians and their supporters against innocent Israeli civilians, while denouncing in extreme terms any retaliatory or defensive moves by the Israeli government and military. Because it is

so one-sided, this left-wing criticism of Israel often crosses the line into blatant anti-Semitism.

And this left-wing anti-Semitism often intertwines the Jews-and-money stereotype as part of its propaganda on behalf of the Palestinian cause. Cartoons from ostensibly liberal sources that depict Jewish power brokers carrying moneybags with which they control Uncle Sam and wreak destruction on innocent Palestinians are published in dozens of European and even some American papers. Some of those who print these cartoons, including college students and other young people, may be only dimly aware of the origins of these vicious images in Nazi mythology and earlier anti-Semitic tradition. Unfortunately, it's all too easy for activists of every political persuasion to reach for the easy emotional lure of hatred when advocating their favored cause.

Still another fountain of anti-Semitic hate—including vicious stereotyping—can be found among many members and supporters of the Nation of Islam, the so-called Black Muslim movement.

In the previous chapter, I mentioned the once-proud alliance between African Americans and Jews in support of civil rights, which has now become a sadly forgotten chapter of history for too many people. In the last two decades, while many Jews and African Americans continue to have warmly positive and friendly personal relationships, on both the community level and among public leaders of these two minority groups, steadfast solidarity has largely given way to suspicion, mistrust, and occasionally outright hostility.

Stereotyped images related to Jews and money have played a significant role in creating and shaping this sense of tension between the African American and Jewish communities. Bayard Rustin, the famed civil rights leader and director of the A. Philip Randolph Institute, examined the reasons for this tension in a famous speech he delivered at the 55th National Commission Meeting of ADL on May 6, 1968, titled "The Anatomy of Frustration."

As Rustin explained, the average struggling black person living in inner-city America in the 1960s would probably know four kinds of white people: police officers, business owners, schoolteachers, and social workers. And all four tended to be sources of frustration, humiliation, and anger for the black citizen—despite the fact that most of these whites were living and working in the inner city with purely innocent, even noble intentions. Furthermore, as Rustin pointed out, in many American cities, three of those four archetypal white figures were likely to be Jewish (all except the police officer).

Rustin's analysis of the role of the schoolteacher in the urban community was typical—and unfortunately still largely accurate:

> In the ghetto, one does not analyze that the Board of Education and the whole system is corrupt, that no matter how much that teacher wants to teach she cannot teach in those conditions. One does not bother to analyze that it is not the

teacher's fault that the child has no breakfast, and may not have lunch, that he may have to go to the poolroom to bum money for potato chips and an orange soda and that that may be all he eats that day. How can you teach that child? How can you teach children when you have forty in a class and two disruptive children who need psychiatric care? To the ghetto mother, there is the teacher and she is Jewish. And she doesn't think the Jewish teacher cares whether her child gets to learn or not.

The unhappy result of this breakdown in understanding: Many African Americans came to identify Jews with the "white oppressors" responsible for their economic and social problems. From this, it was an easy step to accepting many of the anti-Semitic stereotypes about Jews and money, especially the notion that Jews control the economy and use that power to exploit the less fortunate—in particular, African Americans.

A lot has changed in America since the late 1960s. The Jewish presence in African American neighborhoods has greatly diminished, and a growing black middle class has reached new heights of economic, political, and professional achievement. Yet despite these changes, the anti-Semitic assumptions that found fertile ground among African Americans have lingered, along with the political, economic, and social frustrations that helped to feed them. Thus, among at least a significant minority of African Americans, anti-Semitism remains a potent emotional and intellectual force.

One of the forces most responsible for fueling the continued existence of anti-Semitic feeling in the African American community has been the Nation of Islam (NOI). The organization's current leader, Louis Farrakhan, has been a promoter since 1984 of a host of bizarre and ugly conspiracy theories and attacks on Jews, including, for example, claims that Jewish doctors deliberately infected black children with diseases. In 1991, the Nation of Islam published an anonymous book titled *The Secret Relationship Between Blacks and Jews,* which has much in common with that earlier fabrication, *The Protocols of the Learned Elders of Zion.* In this pseudo-scholarly tome (containing no fewer than 1,275 footnotes!), it is claimed that Jews were the *dominant* economic force behind the slave trade that brought millions of Africans in chains to the New World. A typical passage from *The Secret Relationship* reads:

> The Jewish Caribbean presence began in earnest with Columbus' initial foray into the region. With these early Jewish colonists the economic motivation for the exploitation of millions of Black Americans was introduced to the Western Hemisphere. The strategy seemed simple enough . . . wealth would be amassed through a plantation economy driven by sugar cane. . . . [T]he history of the industry became entwined with the western migration of the Jews. They were primarily the financiers and merchants and in a few instances they were also the plantation masters. Jews from Portugal, Holland, England and all over Europe advantaged themselves

through the domination of the commerce of these island regions, particularly in sugar.

Jewish slave traders procured Black Africans by the tens of thousands and funneled them to the plantations of South America and throughout the Caribbean. There remains no documented trace of protest over this behavior. . . . it was a purely commercial venture with which Judaism did not interfere. Whether the local influence was Portuguese, Dutch or English, the Black man and woman fared the same. In Curaçao in the seventeenth century, as well as in the British colonies of Barbados and Jamaica in the eighteenth century, Jewish merchants played a major role in the slave trade. In fact, in all the American colonies, whether French (Martinique), British, or Dutch, Jewish merchants frequently dominated.

So popular is this farrago that Henry Louis Gates, the distinguished professor who heads the W. E. B. Du Bois Institute for African and African American Research at Harvard, denounced *The Secret Relationship* as "the Bible of the new anti-Semitism."

Were there actually any Jews among the many slave traders who created and maintained the tragic, shameful practice that is such a blot on American and world history? Yes, there were some—and their existence, far from being some kind of secret suppressed by a Jewish conspiracy, has been thoroughly documented by genuine scholars. Historian Saul S. Friedman, for example, is one of several experts who have examined the extensive documentary evidence about Jewish involvement in slavery. His conclusions: Jews owned less than 0.03 percent of all the slaves in America; less than 2 percent of the 600,000 slaves imported to the United States were handled by Jewish traders; and less than 1 percent of the ten million slaves imported to other countries in the New World involved Jews.

In short, the participation of Jews in the slave trade—while deplorable—was minimal. It would appear that the purpose of *The Secret Relationship* was not to set the historical record straight but rather to stir up hostility between the black and Jewish communities by retailing a new variation on old anti-Semitic stereotypes—specifically, by claiming that Jewish merchants were so greedy and ruthless that they far outcompeted Christian traders when it came to trafficking in human beings. Like the other versions of the Jewish money canard, it's simply not true.

Anti-Semitism in the Nation of Islam isn't merely backward-looking. Farrakhan is also an active promoter of myths about Jews and money currently. A series of lectures by Farrakhan in early 2010, rife with conspiracy theories about Jews and Israel, and Jewish control of government, finance, and Hollywood, leave little doubt that anti-Semitism and racism remain a central part of his message. The series of three speeches, beginning with his February 28 Saviors' Day speech and culminating with an address on March 14 at Mosque Maryam in Chicago, put Farrakhan's use of anti-Semitism on full display. Farrakhan accused some Jews of belonging to a "synagogue of Satan," asserted that Jews control the entertainment industry and exploit black performers for their own financial gain, and repeated the lie that Jews were disproportionately involved in the transatlantic slave trade. Some of the more blatantly anti-Semitic slurs from Farrakhan's recent speeches include:

- "The Federal Reserve is the synagogue of Satan, the Rockefellers, the DuPonts, the House of Rothschild, these are the people that have corrupted the entire world."—Speech at Mosque Maryam, Chicago, March 14, 2010

- "The Black man and woman have always been looked upon as the 'property' of White America; and particularly, members of the Jewish community. They've always looked at you as 'belonging' to them."—Speech at Mosque Maryam, Chicago, March 7, 2010

- "The Jewish people have said that Hollywood is theirs. Can any of you deny that they are the masters of Hollywood, where sex, lesbianism, homosexuality and violence are promoted?"—Speech at Mosque Maryam, Chicago, March 7, 2010

- "Who owns the recording companies? People who call themselves 'Jews,' but they are not Jews; they are masquerading. . . . And the so-called Jews who run those record companies . . . they use you, and they've sent you all over the world degrading the culture of other nations with your filth and debauchery."—Speech at Mosque Maryam, Chicago, March 7, 2010

Every so often, we see reports in the mainstream media suggesting that Farrakhan has "matured" or "mellowed" and that the message of hate the Nation of Islam once promoted is now a thing of the past. I wish it were so, but the evidence suggests quite the opposite.

In fact, as this book was being readied for press, Minister Louis Farrakhan opened a new chapter in his ministry that suggests that scapegoating Jews is no longer just part of a message, but *the* message.

On June 24, 2010, Farrakhan sent a letter to me, with copies to numerous other American Jewish leaders, along with copies of a new, two-volume edition of *The Secret Relationship Between Blacks and Jews.* Accusing Jews of being guilty of "the most vehement anti-Black behavior in the annals of our history in America and the world," the letter extended an offer of dialogue to "help me in the repair of my people from the damage that has been done by your ancestors to mine."

The letter was sent in advance of a sold-out speech given by Farrakhan on June 26 to thousands of followers at the Atlanta Civic Center in Atlanta, Georgia, in which he announced his intention to present the newly written anti-Semitic book to Jewish leaders on behalf of the Nation of Islam. Like the book itself, Farrakhan's speech was rife with conspiracy theories about Jewish control of government, finance, and Hollywood.

Here is just a sampling from Farrakhan's speech:

> The Rothschilds became rich from cotton, the Lehman brothers became rich from cotton in Alabama, then moved to New York and Wall Street. I know the truth. And somebody gotta tell it or die trying. . . .
>
> Do you know that in Europe in every nation where they were, they led an industry in commerce in trade in banking? And the gentiles were angry with them because everywhere they went, they ruled. So the gentiles rose up against the Jews and persecuted them in Europe. . . .
>
> I'm here to tell you no black man or woman becomes a multimillionaire without friendship in the Jewish community. . . . Did you know that nearly all prominent Negro actors and musicians have or had Jewish sponsors and managers? . . . They have a way of attaching themselves to your gifts, but you get nothing. They get it all.

Of course, his offer of "dialogue" was disingenuous at best. Dialogue does not begin with bigoted accusations. Never in our twenty years of monitoring the statements of Minister Farrakhan have we seen him so obsessed with the alleged misdeeds of the Jews. Yet thousands of people and many in the media continue to treat him as a respectable community spokesman. One wonders why there aren't more voices in the African American community willing to stand up and firmly reject Farrakhan's hatred and his anti-Semitism. When will good people in the community be courageous enough to declare, "Enough already"?

There are also disturbing signs that familiar anti-Semitic canards are infecting some members of the so-called Tea Party movement, the loose and rapidly evolving network of antigovernment activists that has arisen since the 2008 election.

For example, in the run-up to a Tea Party protest held in San Mateo, California, on April 15, 2009, an organization calling itself the Bay Area Ron Paul Campaign for Liberty created a promotional Web site replete with anti-Semitic imagery, such as a picture of a bucket of money being poured into a funnel with a Star of David on it. This funnel, in turn, dripped blood onto a person holding a Palestinian flag, who appeared to be drowning in blood. The text underneath this image read, "Uncle Sam Reminds You: KEEP PAYING TAXES. The ongoing extermination of Palestinian Children Can't Be Done Without Your Help."

Similarly, on November 5, 2009, some five thousand activists gathered in Washington, D.C., to hold a Tea Party protest against Democratic plans to reform the U.S. health insurance system. According to media reports, members of the crowd held up one banner depicting Holocaust victims with the words "National Socialist Healthcare, Dachau, Germany, 1945" and another with the slogan "Obama takes his orders from the Rothchilds [sic]." Holocaust comparisons are dicey business in the best of circumstances; to use an image of murdered Jews to imply that health care reform bears any similarity at all to Nazi tyranny is obviously beyond the pale. And quite obviously the accusation that the U.S. president is under the thumb of Jewish European bankers is a classic anti-Semitic slur (whose relevance to the health care debate is questionable at best).

This was no obscure gathering: The rally was addressed by a number of political luminaries who apparently hoped to curry favor with the Tea Partiers—and to attract votes from the movement they represent. It's a worrisome symptom of our nation's political climate when mainstream figures, including members of Congress, participate in an event that countenances such extreme—and dangerous— attitudes.

The festering pools of anti-Semitic infection on the fringes of American and world civilization would be disturbing enough—after all, they have an impact, direct or indirect, on the thinking of millions of people. Yet in somewhat less blatant form, hateful stereotypes about Jews and money have also seeped into the mainstream culture, where they are reflected in thoughtless remarks by public figures and images and storylines in the mass media.

Some instances of the spread of anti-Semitic beliefs into unexpected cultural corners are very peculiar. For example, the ADL was alerted to an article titled "Money Matrix" in—of all things—the November 2009 issue of a magazine called *Urban Garden,* which is mainly dedicated to extolling the benefits of organic farming and similar topics. A sidebar to the article headed "Who Owns the Federal Reserve?" listed nine private banks, many bearing Jewish names—a typical presentation derived from age-old anti-Semitic conspiracy theories suggesting that the Federal Reserve is "controlled by Jews." The inclusion of this list in an article on the origins of money and lending only gives new credence and legitimacy to this long-held anti-Semitic conspiracy theory, whether or not that support was intended.

Of course, the theory is as fallacious as it is commonplace. The Federal Reserve is a U.S. government institution and is not "owned" by any private entities. The reserve system is composed of twelve major banks created by acts of Congress, and its Board of Governors is similarly legislatively created and subject to congressional oversight. The Rothschilds have nothing to do with it!

To their credit, the editors of *Urban Garden* removed the sidebar from their magazine's Web site shortly after the ADL alerted them to its erroneous nature and its dubious provenance. But the fact that it ever appeared in the pages of a horticultural magazine illustrates how widespread the myths beloved by anti-Semites have become.

In other cases, people who should know better repeat silly stereotypes about Jews with the intention, not of slandering, but of *complimenting* them.

In 2007, for example, former Wisconsin governor Tommy Thompson was speaking before a group of political activists when he uttered the following remark: "I'm in the private sector and for the first time in my life I'm earning money. You know that's sort of part of the Jewish tradition and I do not find anything wrong with that." We know for a fact that Thompson didn't intend to slander Jews with these words—first, because of the audience he was addressing (Thompson was making a speech at the Religious Center of Reform Judaism in Washington, D.C.), and second, because of the circumstances (Thompson was in the midst of exploring a possible presidential bid). Thompson was courting public support, not trying to alienate people—which means he somehow believed that repeating an age-old stereotype about Jews and money would *please* his Jewish listeners!

There could be no more vivid illustration of how deeply ingrained these stereotypes have become. Many non-Jews take them so completely for granted that they use them without even stopping to think how they must sound in Jewish ears—a startling and frankly rather depressing fact. The occasional, often seemingly unconscious use by thoughtless people of an offensive phrase like "Jewing down" (referring to haggling over price or trying to get a bargain) is another symptom of the same phenomenon—the phrase is so much a part of the language for many people that they may not even fully realize that it refers in an insulting fashion to a particular ethnic and religious group. And still another symptom is the habit among many youngsters of using forms of mockery based on derisive stereotypes—for example, taunting sports opponents by tossing pennies in their direction. (The "joke" is that a Jew will supposedly be distracted from the game and will stop to greedily gather the coins.) I hear complaints about this kind of taunting distressingly often. How sad that parents will raise their children in a home where ethnic and religious hostility is taken for granted and even considered a source of amusement.

A recent instance of ingrained stereotyping occurred in October 2009, when a couple of Republican county chairmen in South Carolina penned a newspaper op-ed column in support of a fellow Republican, conservative senator Jim DeMint. Edwin Merwin and Jim Ulmer wrote in their op-ed, "There is a saying that the Jews who are wealthy got that way not by watching dollars, but instead by taking care of the pennies and the dollars taking care of themselves." Their intention was to laud the notion of fiscal responsibility, but instead they evoked ancient images of Jews as both rich and miserly. The gaffe was offensive and completely unnecessary, since the basic idea didn't call for any reference to Jews or any other ethnic group.

Senator DeMint quickly disowned the op-ed, calling the comment thoughtless and hurtful, and Merwin and Ulmer soon apologized. I strongly doubt that any of these three men have any anti-Semitic attitudes. The fact that they stumbled so easily into using offensive stereotypes illustrates how pervasive these stereotypes are, as well as the need for much more general education about them.

And you know that a stereotyped image of Jews has truly gone global when it is part of the daily cultural currency in a country where there are few Jews. Journalist Evan Osnos recently observed this surprising prevalence of people complimenting the Jews by stereotyping them in—of all places—China. Osnos describes a Chinese magazine article headlined "Do the Jews Really Control America?" that recounts the usual stereotyped notions about Jews dominating U.S. industry, finance, and media. But then, Osnos reports, the article "takes a distinctly Chinese turn: the author answers his titular question with a hopeful yes, noting that the Jewish people—known to be 'permeated with wisdom, full of wit and talent'—the people who gave us Einstein, Freud, Marx, Spielberg—occupy a healthy position of influence in America." In other words, according to Osnos, the Chinese evidently agree that the Jews control America—and they are happy about it.

It's nice, I suppose, that the Chinese regard us Jews as wise, witty, and talented. But the notion that Jews control America is at best a two-edged sword. What happens when the United States takes actions that conflict with Chinese interests? Will the Jews get credit or blame for those? Two thousand years of painful history make it all too obvious that even supposedly benign stereotypes are often merely the prelude to yet another round of scapegoating when things go badly—as, eventually, they always do.

And make no mistake, today's troubled economic landscape of-fers an all-too-perfect opportunity for just such scapegoating—not just by extreme hatemongers or Internet bloggers from society's lu-natic fringe, but even, at times, by figures from the mainstream media whose ideas and attitudes influence millions of their fellow citizens.

One example that created quite a bit of controversy in early 2010 involved perhaps the single most influential conservative com-mentator in the United States, radio host Rush Limbaugh.

On January 21, Limbaugh decided to address the then-current controversy over proposals by the Democratic administration in Washington to impose stricter regulations on the banking industry. The main goal would be to try to prevent any recurrence of the fi-nancial meltdown of 2008–2009 by discouraging bankers from tak-ing excessive risks with investors' and depositors' money. Tighter regulations on business are generally opposed by conservatives and Republicans like Limbaugh, and undoubtedly the partisan commen-tator felt that this issue was one for which he could make a strong political point by criticizing President Barack Obama. In particular, he may have felt that Obama was politically vulnerable at the mo-ment as indicated by straws in the wind, like the surprise victory on January 19, 2010, of Republican Scott Brown in the battle for the Senate seat long held by Democrat Ted Kennedy.

All of that is perfectly legitimate, part of the perennial give-and-take among political opponents. But the way Limbaugh expressed his ideas was not legitimate. He told his listeners: "To some people, banker is a code word for Jewish; and guess who Obama is assaulting? He's assaulting bankers. He's assaulting money people. And a lot of those people on Wall Street are Jewish. So I wonder if there's— if there's starting to be some buyer's remorse there."

It's not completely clear what Limbaugh was trying to accomplish with these comments. (If he was hoping to appeal to Jewish listeners by accusing Obama of "assaulting" their fellow Jews on Wall Street, it seems like a lame approach—how would evoking a repulsive stereotype about Jews help to win their hearts and minds?) But regardless of its political effectiveness, Limbaugh's casual reliance on the equation "Bankers = Jews" (despite his clumsy attempt to attribute it to "some people" rather than taking responsibility for it) served to reinforce some of the worst prejudices that a portion of his audience undoubtedly shares.

As we often do when we become aware of an offensive act by a prominent public figure, the ADL issued a statement on January 21, 2010, criticizing Limbaugh's remarks. We wrote:

> Rush Limbaugh reached a new low with his borderline anti-Semitic comments about Jews as bankers, their supposed influence on Wall Street, and how they vote.
>
> Limbaugh's references to Jews and money in a discussion of Massachusetts politics were offensive and inappropriate. While the age-old stereotype about Jews and money

has a long and sordid history, it also remains one of the main pillars of anti-Semitism and is widely accepted by many Americans. His notion that Jews vote based on their religion, rather than on their interests as Americans, plays into the hands of anti-Semitic conspiracy theorists.

When he comes to understand why his words were so offensive and unacceptable, Limbaugh should apologize.

To be perfectly clear, I did *not* accuse Rush Limbaugh of anti-Semitism, nor did I call him an anti-Semite. (I've dealt with these issues long enough to have developed strong sensitivities about using language with great care and precision.) In the ADL statement, I referred to Limbaugh making "borderline anti-Semitic comments," which I think is exactly right. I condemned the comments—not Rush Limbaugh the man. Nor did I accuse Limbaugh of being "an anti-Semitic conspiracy theorist"; rather, I pointed out that his comments "played into the hands" of such theorists. It's an important distinction that at the ADL we tried to make precisely. It's discouraging to find it ignored or distorted.

As a spokesperson for the battle against intolerance, I would have a big problem if I were to apply my standards of judgment in a biased or slanted fashion. For example, if I rushed to condemn offensive or bigoted statements by conservatives while ignoring or condoning similar statements by liberals, I would quickly forfeit the ADL's credibility—and the same is true in reverse, of course. I don't think anyone can credibly accuse me of such bias. When I look back at the loudest controversies I've been embroiled in over the years, I see both conservatives and liberals, Democrats and Republicans, on both sides of the issues. I haven't hesitated to criticize leaders, spokespeople, and commentators of every political stripe—nor have I refused to offer forgiveness and support to those who sincerely apologize for past mistakes and work to change their ways.

What I worry about, however, is that the underlying point may get lost in the focus on a personal and political controversy. Whether you're a liberal or a conservative, a Republican or a Democrat, I hope you can agree with me that repeating, reinforcing, and trafficking in offensive stereotypes about Jews (or any other group) is both ignorant and wrong. And it's not justified because it's sometimes a handy way of scoring a quick political point. The problem of bigotry is too important for us to play games with.

In commenting on this in his *Forward* column, J. J. Goldberg reviewed my history of run-ins with critics from both sides of the political spectrum, noting that I angered the left by criticizing Jesse Jackson's use of the word "Hymietown" and by accepting an apology from conservative Christian leader Pat Robertson after he used bigoted imagery—then angered the right by subsequently denouncing a Robertson video that depicted Jews as Christ-killers and by publicly declaring my continuing friendship with Jackson. Goldberg concluded:

The fact is that Foxman has been going after right and left alike with more or less equal gusto for decades, charging antisemitism when he thinks he sees it and publicly rejecting the charge when he thinks it's unfounded. . . .

In the end Foxman seems to embody for each critic whatever it is that the critic most dislikes about Jewish advocacy, whether for being too liberal or too conservative, too militant or too pragmatic.

While it is a hopeful sign that relatively few Americans openly and deliberately embrace anti-Semitic stereotypes today, it's disturbing that so many people have absorbed biased beliefs about Jews and money to the point where they don't even realize that these beliefs are false, bigoted, and offensive.

Occasionally I encounter people who wonder why I am so concerned about the persistence of ethnic stereotyping aimed at Jews. Isn't it human nature to make assumptions about people—a quick and easy way of reducing the complexity of life to manageable proportions? And if a few uninformed or poorly educated people take these oversimplified assumptions a bit too seriously, what's the harm really?

The implication behind questions like these, which are sometimes asked by well-intentioned people, is that I and others who share my concerns are exaggerating the significance of anti-Semitic stereotyping. And often lurking behind this attitude is another assumption that is itself a form of stereotyping—the belief that Jews are simply "too sensitive" about anti-Semitism and that, if only they would stop "whining" about the problem, it would go away.

I'd like to believe that anti-Semitic stereotyping isn't a real problem. Unfortunately, the facts don't permit that conclusion. I can't help thinking, for example, of the Ilan Halimi case that rocked French society just a few years ago.

Ilan Halimi was a young French Jew of Moroccan heritage who worked as a shop clerk and lived in one of the tough, working-class neighborhoods of Paris known as the *banlieues*. In January 2006, he was lured to an apartment block where a vicious youth gang calling themselves The Barbarians was waiting. They kept Halimi imprisoned for twenty-four days, during which time they subjected him to unspeakable tortures—stabbing, burning, beating, even being set on fire. Finally, on February 13, he was discovered naked, bound, and handcuffed to a tree near a suburban railroad track, his body covered with wounds as well as burns from acids and flammable liquids. He died on his way to the hospital.

The case sparked horror and outrage among decent French citizens of every background. Tens of thousands, including prominent government and religious leaders, joined protest marches decrying gang brutality. Law enforcement officials moved aggressively in response. Twenty-seven members of The Barbarians were arrested in connection with the kidnapping and murder of Halimi, and as of this writing nineteen have been convicted and sent to prison. The group's self-proclaimed leader, Youssouf Fofana, is serving a life sentence.

And what does all this have to do with anti-Semitic stereotyping? Just this: Based on statements by the gang members themselves, it seems clear that Ilan Halimi was kidnapped, tortured, and killed specifically because he was a Jew. According to Nicolas Sarkozy—then the interior minister of France, today the country's president—gang members told police they chose Halimi because they "knew" that all Jews are wealthy, and that kidnapping a Jew and holding him for ransom was an easy route to riches.

Sure enough, soon after Halimi disappeared, his family members began receiving phone calls demanding a fortune in ransom money—450 thousand euros to be exact. It was an absurd sum to request from a poor working-class family—but in the minds of the aptly named Barbarians, who had swallowed many of the anti-Semitic stereotypes I've discussed, there was no such thing as a "working-class Jew." It seems likely that the gang members' rage on discovering that no cash windfall was forthcoming as a result of their crime helped fuel their insane violence toward young Halimi.

Are we Jews "too sensitive" when it comes to anti-Semitic stereotypes? I don't think so. When we consider hate crimes like this one, we realize all too clearly that stereotypes can kill—not figuratively, but literally.

As we've seen in this chapter, the myths about Jews and money have attracted believers around the world, on all sides of the political spectrum, and even in places where Jews themselves are scarcely known. And the power of these myths persists even in an age when more people than ever understand the evil and destructive potential of bigotry. One reason is the availability of a new set of technological tools that can and should be used to spread information, understanding, and wisdom but that all too often are employed for disseminating hatred. In the next chapter, we'll examine these tools and their troubling impact on our culture.

5

WHEN
EVERYONE
HAS A
MEGAPHONE

Let's pause to consider what I've explored so far.

As we've seen, the historic social and psychological bias that is anti-Semitism has three main component beliefs or attitudes that reinforce one another. The first is the accusation of deicide—the belief, deeply rooted in Christian teaching, that Jews rejected and killed Jesus Christ and in so doing committed the greatest crime in the history of humankind: the murder of God. The second is the suspicion of disloyalty—the belief that Jews, no matter where they may live or what citizenship they may hold, are never faithful members of any society but rather are inherently selfish, concerned only with the well-being of themselves and their fellow Jews, and therefore constantly prone to treachery. And the third pillar of anti-Semitism is the assumption that Jews have a unique, and uniquely evil, relationship to money—that they will sacrifice all other interests in the pursuit of wealth and that, as a result of this centuries-old obsession, they have come to amass an incredible amount of economic power that they use, in secret, to manipulate the world into doing their bidding.

All three of these beliefs, in various forms, are part of the classic syndrome of anti-Semitism. They all played roles in shaping and fueling the racist doctrines of Nazi Germany and in motivating the Holocaust. And they are all found, in varying admixtures, in the teachings of hate groups and extremist organizations the world over, from the neo-Nazi and militia movements of the American far right to ultranationalist organizations in Europe to anti-Zionist groups in the Middle East and elsewhere that attack, not specific Israeli policies, but rather the legitimacy of the very idea of a state where Jews can live in peace and security.

And, sadly, all three of these pillars of anti-Semitism have also infiltrated mainstream cultures around the world, as reflected not only in folk beliefs, stories, jokes, and popular imagery, but also in literature, movies, television, journalism, and the official propaganda of some governments.

In these mainstream channels, anti-Semitic beliefs may not appear as virulent, extreme, and dangerous as they do in fringe publications such as *The Protocols of the Learned Elders of Zion* or the speeches of hatemongers like Nation of Islam leader Louis Farrakhan. At a glance, they may even appear relatively harmless: an unflattering caricature of a Jewish character in a movie or play; a few wisecracks about Jewish stinginess in a comedian's routine; a reference to the "bloodthirsty Jewish mob" in an Easter sermon; a comparison of the treatment of Palestinian refugees by Israeli officials to the murder of

Jews by the Nazis in a politician's speech. All of these forms of soft, mainstream anti-Semitism may be, and sometimes are, presented by people who truly consider themselves free of bigotry and who would sincerely protest that "Some of my best friends are Jewish!"

I do not equate these kinds of offensive statements and images with the hatemongering of a Hitler, a Farrakhan, or even a Henry Ford. But it's a mistake to regard them as harmless. Precisely because they are so commonplace and so thoroughly integrated into the language of mainstream society, they serve as fertile soil in which more potent and deadly forms of bigotry can take root and grow. Children who grow up hearing casual, thoughtless expressions of bias and bigotry from the adults around them, or in the classroom at school, or from the pulpit on Sunday, often become adults who "know," without thinking much about it, that Jews are somehow untrustworthy, deceitful, and mean. They "know" this in the same way we all "know" things that were in the air as we were growing up—that George Washington never told a lie, that elephants never forget, that pirates wore eye patches and said "Arrrr," and that lightning never strikes twice in the same place.

People who grow up surrounded by casual anti-Semitism—as we all do, to some extent—and never learn to question it are prone to notice and remember "facts" and experiences that fit their inherited assumptions about Jews, and to ignore and forget others that don't. If a shopkeeper with a Jewish-sounding name refuses to give a person a refund to which he or she feels entitled, that person is likely to chalk it up to "typical Jewish greediness," while never reflecting on the dozens of times he or she has been treated with courtesy and consideration by other people with similar names.

And if a person someday is in a situation in which blaming Jews is a psychologically convenient way of rationalizing an uncomfortable situation, the individual may find that doing so is simply the path of least resistance. Why didn't I get that job I applied for?—the Jewish boss must have hired "one of his own kind" instead. Why are my taxes so high?—the government is sending too much money to support those imperialist Jews in Israel. Why did the bank turn me down for a loan?—because the Jewish bankers have a stranglehold on world finance. Believing things like this is all too easy if you've been surrounded by similar assumptions your whole life—especially if you've never heard them challenged.

And that is why, in this book and in my work with the Anti-Defamation League, I take all forms of bias and bigotry seriously: not because I consider them all equivalent, nor because (as some have said) I think I see "anti-Semites under every bed," but because I know that ignorance, misunderstanding, and falsehood can have a cumulative effect, creating a climate in which more explosive and dangerous forms of hatred can find acceptance.

Against this backdrop, the special importance of the third pillar of anti-Semitism—the mythology about Jews and money—is readily apparent. In a curious way, this third pillar is the one that is most deeply grounded in everyday life, culture, and folkways.

Most people don't think or talk a lot about the (false) role of the Jews as Christ-killers, except perhaps when they attend a performance of an Easter pageant or a passion play. Even for practicing Christians, the issue of who precisely caused the death of Jesus is mostly a matter of history, not of immediate practical import.

Similarly, the supposed proclivity of Jews to betray their communities and nations in pursuit of their self-interest as Jews is a topic that generally arises, if at all, in discussions of geopolitics— when foreign policy experts debate the relative influence of the pro-Israel and pro-Arab lobbies on the U.S. Congress. These topics, while of intense concern to those of us who care deeply about the security of Israel and the maintenance of strong United States–Israel relationships, aren't exactly everyday topics of discussion around most American kitchen tables, water coolers, or soccer fields.

But money is a topic that everyone thinks about. And in times of economic stress like today, it's one that everyone worries and wonders about. Money is on everyone's mind. Practically everyone could use more of it; we all expend a lot of energy working for it and trying to spend and save it wisely; and we're often confused and troubled by the money-related news that bombards us on TV, radio, the Internet, and in our daily papers. Why did the economy nearly collapse in 2008? What went so badly wrong with the world financial system? What's behind the current slowdown in demand and economic growth? What's the meaning and the potential danger of the deficits our government is running? Are Social Security, our private pensions, and our savings and investment accounts safe and reliable? What kind of economic future will our kids and grandkids experience? These money-related questions and more are keeping millions of people awake at night.

Under these circumstances, the persistence of a framework of ideas that provides a simplistic, black-and-white, and (for many) emotionally appealing explanation of how the world of money *really* works is extremely significant. "Blame the Jews" is a nasty game at the best of times; in the wake of the Great Recession of 2008–2009, it's a positively dangerous one.

―――――――

As I've already noted, the last time our economy was in such straits, during the 1930s, the world witnessed an alarming explosion of anti-Semitic hatred. It took the most lethal form, of course, in Europe. But for a time the United States also flirted seriously with anti-Semitism, and one of the driving forces behind this frightening phenomenon was a powerful new communications medium— radio. At the same time that President Franklin D. Roosevelt in his calming, humane voice was using radio to educate and rally the nation through his famous "fireside chats," Father Coughlin and other right-wing agitators were using the airwaves to spread vicious propaganda blaming minority-group members—especially the Jews—for the troubles America faced.

Thankfully, the wisdom of Roosevelt and other mainstream American leaders prevailed, and the United States did not travel the path toward tyranny that such great and highly educated nations as Germany and Japan followed. But the dangerous appeal of bigotry never dies out permanently. And in today's era of economic turmoil, it is attracting new followers through the power of another new communications medium—the Internet.

One of the most remarkable attributes of the global network of networks that forms the Internet is the power—for good or evil—it gives users to respond almost instantaneously to events on the world stage. A recent example brings this home with chilling force.

In January 2010, a massive earthquake struck the impoverished island nation of Haiti. Flimsy construction meant that hundreds of thousands of homes, schools, and other structures were destroyed within moments. The world looked on in horror and dismay as millions of Haitians became its victims—thousands by sudden death in the immediate aftermath of the quake, many more by shortages of food, water, medicine, and shelter in the weeks that followed.

Dozens of humanitarian groups and aid agencies rushed into action. Almost all used the Internet to rally support, transmit information about the disaster, and collect donations from concerned individuals. But a handful of less-well-intentioned people took advantage of the tragedy and of the reach of the Internet to pursue a very different agenda.

As events were unfolding in Haiti, a relatively unknown blogger and self-appointed YouTube pundit, known only as T. West, took to the airwaves with a message for the people of Port-au-Prince: Earthquake victims beware!

His warning was based on a claim as bizarre as it was outrageous: that the Israelis involved in rendering humanitarian assistance and manning a mobile hospital unit were possibly "harvesting organs" for profit as part of the rescue operation. After all, he insinuated, the Israelis had done it before and could do so again. And the story had an inherent plausibility in the ears of many hearers simply because it meshed with a familiar folk belief—the stereotyped image of Jews as people who will do anything, no matter how cruel and inhumane, for the sake of a dollar.

There was once a time when this kind of unfounded conspiracy theory would have found no audience beyond the messenger's small cadre of followers. But today's Internet is a kind of Wild Wild West where any unfounded or outrageous accusation can reach a global audience—and assume a patina of truth.

The Israeli "organ harvesting" conspiracy theory YouTube video was picked up and reported as fact by, among others, such far-flung entities as the official state-funded news channel of Iran and the news site of an armed wing of the Palestinian terrorist group Hamas.

The worldwide soapbox of the Internet has made it easy for anyone to "broadcast yourself," as the YouTube slogan goes. And while most people use the Internet for benign purposes, others use it with nefarious intent and without fear of the consequences. Extremists were among the first to recognize the Internet's potential as a powerful megaphone for recruitment and for spewing hatred, and have continued to be on the cutting edge of exploiting its use. Because of the technological power of the medium, any spurious allegation or rumor posted online can be repeated, spread, and embraced as fact within minutes.

Not so long ago, the chief problem areas on the Internet were viral e-mails—messages containing scurrilous legends or accusations passed along by the thousands in ever-multiplying networks of friends and acquaintances—as well as Web sites and blogs, often used by bigoted individuals and organizations to recruit supporters and spread lies. Today, a new arena of Web-spread hatred has opened up. User-driven social-networking sites like YouTube, Facebook, MySpace, Twitter, and many others are proving to be a boon not only to those who put them to use for positive purposes—for sharing news and video clips from the 2009 prodemocracy protests in Iran, for example—but also to those who spread incitement, malicious rumors, extremism, and hatred.

And because the Internet is so wide open—uncontrolled by government licensing, unconstrained by the corporate policies and social mores that moderate the behavior of participants in the mainstream broadcasting and publishing industries—the messages spread via this universal new medium are correspondingly unrestrained. On the Internet you can say anything—and get away with it.

Thus, if stereotypes about Jews and money are currently reflected in subtle form in the mass media, they are broadcast in not-so-subtle form on the Internet and among hate groups. The communications revolution has blurred the lines between what is mainstream and what is not, making it easy for people and groups with extremist views to communicate more easily, continuously, and widely.

The Internet also facilitates the continual recirculation of false or bigoted statements and information. If a newspaper, TV network, or radio station publishes some outlandish untruth, its impact is usually somewhat limited. Not so with the Internet. Even after a phony news story is quickly debunked, it remains available forever on the World Wide Web and often resurfaces endlessly. For some eye-opening examples of how this happens, spend a few minutes visiting Snopes.com, the well-known Web site dedicated to tracking and analyzing "urban legends" that circulate via e-mail and Internet sites.

Barbara Mikkelson and her team of researchers spend countless hours debunking myths—many of them driven by extreme political agendas—that turn up year after year on the Internet, sometimes with dates and other details changed to make them appear current, but otherwise unaltered from the fallacious form in which they originally appeared, sometimes decades earlier.

Furthermore, extremist propaganda was once hard to come by. If you wanted to study the writings of hatemongers (whether anti-Semitic, racist, or what have you), you had to search for them in out-of-the-way bookstores, through the post office boxes of obscure organizations listed in tiny ads in the back of cheap magazines, or at meetings of little-known organizations. Today, hateful speech no longer has to be sought out in furtive corners—it comes to you easily via a Google search or other forms of Web surfing. In fact, many a high school student trying to research a topic like the founding of Israel, the assassination of John F. Kennedy, or the terror attacks of 9/11 for a school term paper has been sucked into the hate sites that appear prominently on search engines, retailing their own perverted versions of "history" as if they were truth.

For all these reasons, the Internet both reflects and perpetuates the hateful underbelly of society and so must be taken seriously.

Today, anti-Jewish invective and conspiracy theories are spreading globally in the United States, in European and Latin American countries, and throughout the Middle East as a result of the global economic crisis. Conspiracy theories linking Jews and Israel to the world financial meltdown are finding a whole new generation of adherents thanks to the power of the Internet.

One widely circulated conspiracy theory suggests that "$400 billion in funds was secretly transferred to Israeli banks" just prior to the collapse of Lehman Brothers and other major investment banks in late 2008. Launched on an anti-Semitic Web site sponsored by a Washington, D.C.–based Holocaust denial publication, this false rumor has ricocheted across the Internet and around the world, appearing on numerous Web sites and comment boards, while few questioned its veracity or examined its origins.

The Nazi propagandists of the 1930s and 1940s would have been thrilled by the Internet—its ability to rapidly disseminate groundless assertions in a form that appears authoritative gives new meaning to the concept of "The Big Lie." Think about the leveling power of the Internet: Even an unsophisticated person can recognize at a glance the difference between a printed copy of the *New York Times* or *Time* magazine and a propaganda rag published by a neo-Nazi club or extremist Muslim sect. The mainstream publication is well printed, attractive, filled with expensive ads, sold on newsstands everywhere, and stocked in public libraries; the propaganda rag is blurry, printed on cheap paper, devoid of ads, and distributed only by seedy-looking characters on street corners. But on a computer screen, all these publications may look more or less the same.

There are disturbing similarities between the "$400 billion" conspiracy theory and the myth that spread around the world after 9/11—the belief that "4,000 Jews" did not report for work the day of the attack on the World Trade Center, having been secretly warned in advance by the Mossad or some other Israeli agency that planned the whole thing. Even today this myth is believed by many around the world. Both stories illustrate the same sad truth: Whenever world events are difficult to explain or understand, Jews serve as a convenient scapegoat.

This belief that only Jews could be responsible for something so catastrophic and damaging to the global economy derives directly from some of the worst anti-Semitic stereotypes. As we've seen, the idea that there is Jewish control of the banking system and the world economy has its antecedents in the *Protocols of the Learned Elders of Zion* and many other forms of anti-Semitic propaganda. And the notion that Jews would happily destroy the world economy if it benefited them nicely links the Jews-and-money stereotypes to the Jew-as-traitor image that is another of the chief pillars of anti-Semitism. What a neat, predictable, and utterly terrifying world it must be for the bigots who believe this stuff.

In the wake of the financial crisis of 2008–2009, the ADL monitored the spread of anti-Semitic expressions around the world. Many appeared on Web sites as articles or comments from individuals, often unidentified, who were angry and seeking to place blame for the spreading impact of the crisis. Some of the articles were accompanied by vicious anti-Semitic caricatures and drawings, deploying the whole range of traditional imagery for depicting Jews as monsters: gigantic hooked noses, fanglike teeth (often dripping blood), hands like the claws of birds of prey, and so on.

Here is just a sampling of the global anti-Semitic reaction that emerged as a result of the ongoing financial crisis. (Not only have we selected just a few of the many hate-filled messages we spotted, but our survey was undoubtedly very incomplete since many Web sites sponsored by reputable publishers and organizations are routinely edited and purged of their more vicious contents.) The samples that follow are organized by country of origin, but of course they are generally all accessible from anywhere in the world—such is the global reach of the Internet.

United Kingdom. The Web site of the mainstream British newspaper the *Independent* featured in its comments section a post by a visitor identifying himself as "Errol Flynn" that repeated the claim about the alleged $400 billion transfer from Lehman Brothers to Israeli banks. In response to a second article on the economic crisis, another reader commented, "So the banks used to be Jewish-owned . . . has anything changed?" Both posts were eventually removed by the site's administrators.

Russia. The Web site of the newspaper *Pravda* published an article arguing that French, German, and Italian leaders were advocating a bailout of European banks to benefit "Rothschild, Kuhn Loeb, and other banking magnates," a reference to well-known Jewish banking families. The article continued, "The trouble is most of Europe is sick of their Zionist puppet governments, the wrecking of the universities and the flood of third world immigration. Another Hitler, running in a united Europe, could be elected in a heartbeat."

In response, a reader named "Khothla" commented, "Which Jews have looted this money, hang these termites. . . . As Jewish bankers again take aim at Russia, we ought to recognize the danger of the situation for the Russian People, and the American People. History teaches us that Jewish leaders are capable of treachery and genocidal murder."

Germany. Several discussion forums and blogs casually linked the crisis and Jews or repeated anti-Semitic stereotypes of the "money-savvy" and "financially dominating Jew." One comment on Ariva.de, an independent provider of financial news, stated, "When it comes to money Jews are always in the say."

On Freenet, a German Internet discussion forum, one user commented, "World-Jewry Finance grabbed trillions of Euros and Dollars. Among them the Jews Rothschild and Morgan-Stanley. With the trillions they will incite further wars and finance them." The individual identified himself with the moniker "world-jewry finance." Another Freenet commenter, using the name "Ramirez61," observed, "It is clear that the United States will remain the world financial center. After all it is the second home of the world finance jews! Rockefeller, Roth-schild, Lehman Brothers, Goldman-Sachs . . . and many more!" (By the way, John D. Rockefeller, a devout Baptist, would be surprised to see how frequently he and his family have been identified as Jews by anti-Semites who assume that anyone prominent in business circles must have Jewish blood in his veins.)

Spain. Op-eds making reference to Jews and the financial crisis appeared in the daily paper *El Pais.* While the articles did not di-rectly accuse Jews of causing the crisis, the Internet comments sec-tion following the articles contained several anti-Semitic entries. One writer declared, "The crisis is not a financial problem but an economic one. . . . [I]t is what is behind this gruesome scene of sav-age capitalism of the Zionist students of Milton Friedman." An Oc-tober 2008 thread in the comments section of *El Pais* was titled, "The world does not learn and here you have again the crisis caused by the Jews in Banking. Who will reimburse the affected, Israel . . . ? or the Zionists?"

Several Spanish financial Web sites featured articles with anti-Jewish themes, including one on Cincodias.com stating that "Lehman's management board is made up of Jews who were only in-terested in results no matter at what price."

Argentina. "The mechanism through which the Zionist Lobby shatters empires after skinning them has repeated once and again throughout history. . . . In our time, these same families can be observed sucking the blood of the European Union, Russia and even America, the ultimate victim of the banker. Because banking, similar to cancer, ends by destroying the organism that acts as its host." This statement appeared in an October 2008 essay on the blog "Red Patriotica Argentina," which focuses on Argentinean nationalism. The essay claimed that Jews were responsible for economic crises in earlier periods, including Germany in the early 1900s. The Web site also accused the "Jewish Lobby" of being responsible for the financial crisis in the United States.

Similarly, a number of October 2008 posts made by individuals to Argentina Indymedia, a left-wing news Web site tailored to various localities, blamed "Zionist speculators" for the financial crisis. A commenter named "Diego," while seemingly defending Jews from blanket accusations of wrongdoing, nonetheless endorsed the notion that religion or ethnicity was somehow an essential element in the financial crisis, writing, "It is worrisome but . . . it is not a novelty that with each global economic crisis they turn to members of the 'chosen people.' But what is really important is to avoid that people's virulence be directed in mass [en masse] to the Jewish people . . . rather than to the unscrupulous Zionist speculators that act on Wall Street." Another commenter, calling himself "Oligarch," mentioned "Bernanke and his predecessor (and agitator of this debacle) Greenspan, the two Moishes and the hedge of Bernie that always makes money . . . no; I do not believe in witches but [they fly]."

Also in October 2008, the discussion board of a mainstream Argentinean newspaper, *La Nacion,* featured this comment by "Roger 9": "I am not at all surprised that the large Jewish community in the US had 'something' to do with this North American Disaster. We [in Argentina] know it very well (by our own experience with a lot of banks owned by people of that community)."

One further observation about these hateful comments: Occasionally, columnists and others who are inclined to minimize the problem of anti-Semitism have pooh-poohed the significance of compilations like these, saying, in effect, "The fact that most of the bigoted statements quoted come from anonymous comments actually demonstrates how *unimportant* anti-Semitism has become. Everyone knows that the comment pages of most Web sites are filled with weird, ill-informed, and extreme opinions. What matters is what the paid contributors to Web sites, newspapers, and magazines write, since they represent mainstream opinion."

There's a grain of truth in this observation. Certainly I would consider it cause for alarm if official commentators for mainstream news sources—op-ed columnists in the *New York Times,* for example, or pundits appearing nightly on CNN or MSNBC—were to spout bigoted remarks and conspiratorial nonsense comparable to the monstrosities we've just quoted from the Internet. Thankfully, we're not at that point in the history of anti-Semitism.

However, I can't agree that it's safe to disregard the vitriol found in the comments pages on the Internet. There are several good reasons to worry about what we read in these sources.

First, the relative volume of hatemongering related to the Jews-and-money stereotype has increased since the economic downturn. We can agree that unedited comments pages on the Internet represent a glimpse of the unfiltered opinions of some of the worst people in the world. But if that's the case, isn't there cause for concern in the fact that their voices now appear to be louder, bolder, and more numerous than in recent history?

Second, the fact that Internet comment sites presenting the un-mediated feelings of ordinary people are now registering an increased level of anti-Semitic hatred suggests, at least, that such attitudes are gaining currency in the population at large. Like the famous canary in the coal mine, the ravings of a collection of hate-mongers on a Web site may not be significant in themselves, but they are worrisome as a symptom of what may be developing on the fringes of our society, beyond the visibility of most of the main-stream media.

Finally, it concerns me that so many of the online diatribes repeat age-old anti-Semitic stereotypes practically verbatim. All the traditional motifs are there: Jews as bloodsuckers, Jews as conspirators, Jews as secret lords of global banking and capitalism, Jews as gangsters, Jews funneling their ill-gotten gains to support Israel, and so on. This doesn't happen by accident. People using these familiar motifs in 2010 didn't make them up—they learned them from older sources, to which they were introduced by people or organizations they somehow had learned to trust. Thus, it's likely that every individual who takes the time to post an anti-Semitic comment on a Web site represents not merely himself but at minimum a small network of others who have fed and nurtured his bigoted attitudes.

I'd like to be able to disregard the hate messages on the Internet as the empty mouthings of a few impotent cranks. But I can't. I know that teachings like these are the seemingly insignificant wellsprings from which the Timothy McVeighs of the world get their start.

Does this sound far-fetched? Sadly, it's not. Current real-life examples aren't hard to find. For instance, James Von Brunn, the 88-year-old self-proclaimed white supremacist, anti-Semite, and Holocaust denier who carried out the shooting at the U.S. Holocaust Memorial Museum in June 2009, was no neophyte when it came to using the Internet. Not only was he a constant presence on the Web as the host of an anti-Semitic site, but over six years Von Brunn changed his site registration 61 times and changed his hosting service five times. The changes may have been merely administrative, attempts to hide the true ownership of the site, or may have been in response to violations of the terms of service of those Internet providers that at one time provided him a platform. In any case, they illustrate the ease with which those who want to use the Internet as a weapon for spreading hatred can do so—and then cover their tracks at will.

It isn't only blogs and news sites that have become online vehicles for spreading hateful messages. Social networking media are now becoming increasingly significant playgrounds for hatred—and effective recruiting venues for some of our society's most dangerous anti-Semitic and racist organizations.

Researchers at the Digital Hate and Terrorism project of the Simon Wiesenthal Center (SWC) have been tracking this problem. Here's a summary of their latest findings, from the report *Facebook, YouTube +: How Social Media Outlets Impact Digital Terrorism and Hate* (May 2009):

> The greatest increase of digital hate has emerged from Facebook and YouTube. [These sites] have seen a proliferation of extremist use, with 30% of new postings on Facebook alone—with the greatest increase coming from overseas, particularly Europe and the Middle East. Facebook officials have met with the SWC and pledged to remove sites that violate their terms of usage. But with over 200 million users, online bigots have to date outpaced efforts to remove them. Some sites have thousands of friends, thus enabling the message of hate to spread virally. These social networking sites have become so prevalent that some "traditional" hate

groups have begun to develop their own versions, such as New Saxon, "a Social Networking site for people of European descent" produced by a traditional American Neo-Nazi group (National Socialist Movement).

Another hate site, Stormfront (generally considered the first online hate site, starting in 1995) uses their Facebook page to connect thousands of visitors to their main website. The UK considers Stormfront's founder Don Black so dangerous that he was recently among 16 extremists barred from entering Britain.

It's particularly worrisome to discover that Facebook, YouTube, and other social networking sites have become infested by hate groups. Many parents assume that these popular sites, which are owned, maintained, and monitored by corporations, are safe places for their kids to roam. As a result, young people spend countless hours in unsupervised exploration of these sites. Many of the connections they'll encounter are harmless, even laudable—Causes on Facebook, for example, provides ways for people to support worthy missions that range from educating girls in Africa to providing relief to victims of the earthquake in Haiti. But others are far from harmless, as the SWC report details.

The question of how to handle controversial or bigoted speech on the Internet is a complicated one. On the one hand, the world has never seen a more vibrant, compelling marketplace of ideas. On the other, it is becoming increasingly apparent that this remarkable marketplace can be extraordinarily harmful and offensive, and even serve as a recruitment tool for violent groups.

Commercial Internet providers continue to grapple with the issues of how to deal with offensive speech. A huge part of the appeal of the Internet lies in its unlimited diversity—the fact that it provides a megaphone for anyone with a cause to promote, an idea to disseminate, a story to share. But when worthwhile messages are swamped in a sea of muck, the attractiveness of the medium itself begins to decline, and this is bound to be an important issue for the commercial organizations whose business model depends on creating an Internet venue in which people feel safe and comfortable.

Yet the decisions made by the leaders of these organizations are often questionable. One wonders, for example, why the enormously popular Facebook, with a community of about 300 million and growing, refuses to block groups that deny the reality or scope of the Holocaust, while retaining its policy against hosting pictures of women breastfeeding. Similar issues confront every platform built to facilitate communication and community.

The social networking technologies of Web–2.0 have created other new perils too, especially among young people. One result of the proliferation of online social networking has been the growing and troubling phenomenon of cyberbullying—the use of technologies like instant messaging, cell phones, texting, and online networking to harass and intimidate.

Cyberbullying can damage reputations and destroy lives. In November 2008, the problem hit close to home for Floridians, when a group of students in north Naples were suspended for allegedly organizing a "kick a Jew day." It was reported that some students had used the Internet and text-messaging to spread the word. This is not the kind of innocent socializing parents imagine when their kids spend an afternoon chatting with friends via the family computer.

I don't want to appear to be a technological alarmist. As I noted early in this chapter, the Internet is an amazing tool for worldwide communication, education, and networking, and it has already done a lot to open doors of information and knowledge to millions of people around the globe. The vast majority of people online are decent, well-meaning people who use their new electronic communication tools for good purposes, not bad. One hopeful sign: In the 2009 survey of anti-Semitic propensities by ADL, we found a smaller percentage of people who are prone to anti-Semitic beliefs among the population at large than among non-Internet users (12 percent versus 19 percent). This suggests that, on balance, people who use the Internet are better informed and more tolerant than those who do not.

Nonetheless, the proliferation of hateful messages on the Internet remains a real problem, one that demands a thoughtful response from policymakers and ordinary citizens alike—a response that respects both American traditions of freedom and the concern we all share for civility and tolerance.

While the First Amendment protects hate speech except when it takes the form of direct threats against specific people, this does not mean that we should accept hate on the Internet as something we are powerless to confront. There is a role to play for Internet users, Internet companies, educators, and parents. We need to identify and develop practical solutions to the pressing issue of online hate so that the extremists do not get the upper hand. The challenge is how to tame the digital Wild West while adhering to the First Amendment, whose guarantees of freedom protect us all.

In the final chapter of this book, I'll outline some of the steps I'd like to see taken to limit the damage that hatemongers can do, whether on the Internet or elsewhere. It's just part of the broader program of action I favor by which all well-meaning people can work together to relegate anti-Semitism and all other forms of bigotry and hatred to the dustbin of history where they belong.

6
NOT SO
FUNNY

I am holding in my hand a book called *Jewtopia: The Chosen Book for the Chosen People* by two men, Bryan Fogel and Sam Wolfson. Maybe "book" isn't exactly the right word. It's really a compilation, between hard covers, of funny photos, slogans, cartoons, dialogues, wisecracks, and gags about Jews and Judaism. And on the top of the dust jacket, on the right-hand side, is the very first joke: A printed price for the book itself of $25.00, crossed out "by hand" and replaced with the scrawled note, "But for you, $24.99!"

That pretty much sets the tone for the whole book. The comedy—such as it is—is based on touching all the buttons of classic Jewish stereotypes: doting mothers, neurotic young men, frigid wives, inedible kosher foods, and so on. And plenty of the jokes revert to the old Jews-are-cheap, Jews-are-greedy, Jews-are-obsessed-with-money images.

A page filled with supposedly "Actual notes from the Wailing Wall" features the hand-written plea, "Dear Hashem, Please let Aunt Marion come out of surgery okay. But if she doesn't, let me get the majority of her equity and assets."

Sidebars scattered through the book highlight "Shylock's Quick Tips on How to Save a Buck"—typical example: "Barney's, Bloomingdale's, and Saks all give major discounts to their employees. Become friends or family with as many of these employees as possible."

A two-page "quiz" titled "How Cheap a Jew Are You?" lets you rate yourself on a four-part scale: "Spendthrift," "Liberal to Moderate," "Frugal," and "Perpetuating the Stereotype."

And a spread devoted to analyzing the theory "Jews Control the World's Money Supply" "debunks" it by saying, "This is simply not true. Only one Jew controls the world economy. And that Jew is Ben Shalom Bernanke." (A few inches further down the page you can enjoy a badly Photoshopped image of Bernanke apparently dancing in a disco, surrounded by young women who are eagerly pawing him. It could be worse—he could have been shown in a skimpy thong on a beach in Latin America, the way Alan Greenspan is on the facing page.)

If this is your idea of side-splitting humor, you're welcome to it. Personally, I find it a little depressing. And I don't know whether it makes it worse or better that the authors of this stuff—the aforementioned Bryan Fogel and Sam Wolfson—are themselves a couple of apparently nice Jewish boys, and that *Jewtopia* was based on a supposedly very successful stage show that sold out theatres in Los Angeles and New York.

As Fogel and Wolfson would probably say: Oy.

I don't mean to pick on Fogel and Wolfson particularly. They're certainly not the only Jewish humorists to make corny Jewish stereotypes the heart of their act. Jewish comedians have long played a role in reinforcing these stereotypes and unintentionally fostering the hostility they evoke.

The whole topic of Jewish humor and its role in mainstream society, particularly in the United States, is an extraordinarily rich one. From the days of vaudeville to the golden age of television to *Saturday Night Live* and beyond, the Jewish comics, actors, writers, and directors who have played major roles in shaping American humor are almost too numerous to mention. Some of the figures who would probably appear on anyone's list include Fanny Brice, the Marx Brothers, Jack Benny, George Burns, Sid Caesar, Carl Reiner, Woody Allen, Lenny Bruce, Rodney Dangerfield, Neil Simon, Mel Brooks, Joan Rivers, Jackie Mason, Gilda Radner, Billy Crystal, and Jerry Seinfeld. I'll stop here, not because I am running out of names but because you get the point. It's almost easier to list the leading American humorists who are *not* Jewish than to try to name all the ones who are!

This acknowledgment of the huge role that Jews have played in the history of American humor raises the natural question: Is there such a thing as Jewish humor? And if there is—the next question that generations of Jewish elders have asked about everything under the sun—Is it good for the Jews?

To start with the first question: Obviously it would be absurd to say that there is one style of humor that unites all the diverse performers I listed above, not to mention all the other funny Jews we've come to know and love over the decades. (For example, did you know that Peter Sellers of *Pink Panther* fame was Jewish? Another name for the list—one that doesn't fit neatly into any preconceived mold.) But many observers nonetheless have suggested that there is some connecting thread—a shared tone, attitude, or worldview—that underlies a distinctly Jewish way of laughing at oneself and at the world.

Some say that Jewish humor is fundamentally a strategy for fending off the attacks of a hostile world, using cleverness, word play, wit, and irony as weapons. In this view, Jewish humor is a street-smart variation of the love of erudition that has always characterized our people: If the rabbi is a brilliant thinker steeped in religious lore and therefore able to disentangle even the most complicated ethical or moral dilemma, the comedian is a wise guy with so much verbal dexterity he can outsmart any opponent, leaving the anti-Semite wondering what hit him.

Two famous lines from Groucho Marx epitomize this strategy of humor-as-weapon: "I wouldn't want to belong to any club that would have me as a member," and (when his family was forbidden access to the swimming pool at a "restricted" country club) "My daughter's only half-Jewish—can she go in up to her waist?" The first gag upends the snobbery that Jews always had to battle by posing a paradox; the second reveals the ridiculous quality of discrimination by carrying it to its illogical conclusion. In both cases, it's a little harder to imagine taking anti-Semitic snobbery quite so seriously after hearing Groucho deflate it.

Others say that Jewish humor is essentially about the suffering that arises from alienation—about the pain one experiences in a world where one is always an outsider. This may be an appropriate description of, for example, Woody Allen's characteristic pose as the neurotic *nebbish,* so accustomed to rejection that he doesn't know how to take yes for an answer, or the style of TV's Larry David, who denies being a self-hating Jew by saying, "Hey, I may loathe myself, but it has nothing to do with the fact that I'm Jewish." But the brash Mel Brooks, the droll George Burns, or the wacky Gilda Radner?—"alienation" doesn't seem to sum up their comic personalities very well.

But even if it's hard to pin down, lots of people seem to agree that there is *something* distinctive about Jewish humor—so much so that generations of TV and Hollywood performers were warned not to make their movies and shows "too Jewish" lest they alienate mainstream audiences. (One supposedly routine strategy: Infuse scripts with the cleverness of Jewish humor, then hire actors with white-bread looks and appeal—"Write Yiddish, cast British," as the saying went.) If there's no such thing as Jewish humor, then how can a show be "too Jewish"? There's a logical disconnect there somewhere.

So if we assume for the sake of argument that there is a Jewish mode of humor, even if it's difficult to define precisely, how do we answer our second question: Is it good for the Jews?

My answer: It depends.

To me, it's wonderful not just that Jews have contributed so richly to America's tradition of humor (and indeed to all of our performing arts) but that, in recent years, we have become more and more uninhibited about acknowledging that reality, even reveling in it. I like the fact that *Saturday Night Live* alumnus Adam Sandler is a proudly practicing Jew who talks about his faith (and even sings about it, as in his famous "Chanakuh Song"). I'm happy that Jerry Seinfeld, unlike generations of earlier performers, never felt it necessary to change his name—and went on to make the very New York, very Jewish *Seinfeld* into the most popular sitcom in history. (A bit of trivia: Seinfeld's costar Jason Alexander, born Jay Greenspan, *did* change his name—and after touring Israel under the auspices of the Anti-Defamation League, became so inspired to explore his Jewish heritage that he became an ADL spokesman.)

So Jewish humor, like all good forms of humor, is something I definitely appreciate and admire. And the fact that millions of Americans of every background have come to love Jewish humor (and even learn a few Yiddish words in the process) is a fine thing, and likely a potent weapon in the battle against anti-Semitism.

But there is a downside to Jewish humor—and that is when Jewish comedians use ethnic stereotypes as their main source of comedy. It's especially problematic, of course, when those stereotypes are hurtful ones that skirt or even openly embrace the myths that anti-Semites teach.

I'm thinking, for example, of the skinflint played for decades on radio, television, and in movies by Jack Benny. Miserliness wasn't the sum total of Benny's comedic persona—he was also petulant, whiny, vain, and a terrible violinist. (In reality, of course, Benny was a very proficient musician.) But cheapness was certainly Benny's signature trait, and his classic jokes revolved around it: the money vault hidden in an incredibly deep cellar, or Benny responding to the stick-up man's demand, "Your money or your life!" with a long, long silence, broken finally by, "I'm thinking, I'm thinking!"

Funny? Absolutely. Benny milked the persona and the gags it generated for all they were worth, and his shows were regularly among the highest-rated programs on the air. But in retrospect, the humor is a bit embarrassing. It hews so closely to the Jews-as-misers stereotype that it must have fueled or at least reinforced the belief in that stereotype among some non-Jewish Americans. It's all too easy to imagine a gentile fan of Jack Benny making a prejudiced observation about "cheap Jews" and then defending his remark by saying, "Come on, even Jack Benny, a Jew, admits it's true!"

I have a similar problem with the character played by comic Fran Drescher on the popular sitcom *The Nanny*. Petulant and whiny, like Jack Benny (why do some Jews on TV come across that way?), she was also acquisitive, vulgar, flashy, and manipulative—a kind of would-be Jewish American Princess forever pining after the handsome millionaire she hoped would eventually put her in furs and diamonds for life. Like Benny, Drescher was quite funny at times—but more than one scene made me cringe. This is *not* the way I want nice Americans from the Midwest or the South, who may not even know a single Jew, to picture every New York Jew!

Don't misunderstand, I'm not trying to say that Jews on TV or in movies (whether in comedies or dramas) aren't supposed to be recognizably Jewish, or that every Jewish character should be a white-bread Mr. or Ms. America type. There may have been a time when Jewish Americans were so insecure and so eager to assimilate seamlessly into mainstream culture that they were actually *afraid* to appear Jewish in public—let alone in the media. Hence the culture of what writer Marnie Winston-Macauley refers to as *"Shanda fur die Goyim"*—in other words, don't embarrass us by being too Jewish in front of the gentiles!

That's not my point. I'm not uncomfortable with Jack Benny's miser or Fran Drescher's tacky nanny because they are "too Jewish." Nor am I urging Jews to shy away from "laughing at ourselves." Being able to recognize and make humor out of one's human foibles is a strength, not a weakness, and our ability to do that is something to celebrate, not to hide.

If anything, I am saying just the opposite. The miser and the Jewish American Princess aren't "too Jewish" for me—the problem is that they aren't really Jewish at all. The character traits of being cheap, grasping, materialistic, and vulgar aren't actually linked to any one religion or ethnic background. To think that they are and that Jews epitomize those traits is both inaccurate and demeaning. And humor based on these stereotypes isn't particularly clever or creative—it's actually lazy, since it merely presses the buttons of the audience's preconceived biases rather than stimulating any fresh awareness or new understanding.

Sometimes people in the media, such as the famed television producer Norman Lear, justify the humorous use of stereotypes as satire, saying it is designed to expose the ridiculousness of bigotry and thereby discourage rather than encourage it. Lear has always defended his legendary character Archie Bunker (inimitably portrayed in the 1970s sitcom *All in the Family* by actor Carroll O'Connor) by pointing out that the bigoted Archie was so blatantly ignorant that audiences quickly recognized the stupidity of his intolerant attitudes, and by noting that Archie generally got his comeuppance by the end of the show.

Unfortunately, it's very difficult to distinguish "laughing at" bigotry from "laughing with" it and thereby making it feel socially acceptable. A disturbing number of people respond to supposedly humorous bigoted remarks by saying things like "It's funny because it's so true."

Archie Bunker is a case in point. It's true that Archie was depicted as stupid—but then, his liberal and tolerant daughter and son-in-law (whom he frequently called "Meathead") fared hardly any better. And while Archie may have gotten his comeuppance in the sense that his bigoted observations were always shown to be inaccurate, he never really suffered as a result of his foolishness. *All in the Family* episodes generally ended with Archie perched on his favorite reclining chair, calling for his wife Edith to bring him a beer, and appearing generally quite satisfied with his life—and definitely not questioning his warped perceptions of the world.

There's another, more subtle problem with the way Archie Bunker was portrayed. When *All in the Family* debuted, it shocked many critics and TV viewers by its relative frankness. It was the first time a prime-time television comedy in the United States even tried to deal with topics like prejudice and bigotry (as well as other hot-button issues such as premarital sex and the Vietnam War). But in retrospect it's quite clear that Archie's bigotry was actually soft-pedaled by the show's script writers.

A small example: Although Archie *sounded* like a typical bigot, he never used the extremely harsh, ugly racial and ethnic epithets that *real* bigots of his day tended to use. (I mean words like *kike* and the n-word.) Instead, he used milder, sometimes made-up substitutes that put a comic spin on his prejudice—terms like "jungle bunny" for African Americans and "hebe" for Jews.

Undoubtedly this was done in deference to the sensibilities of audiences (and advertisers) at the time, and I'm sure the network censors wouldn't have had it any other way. But the effect was to make Archie's hatefulness appear less serious—in fact, to make him just a little more comic and a little more *lovable* than he would otherwise have been. It's not that Norman Lear or anyone else connected with the show wanted in any way to endorse Archie's intolerance. But treating him as a harmless, comic foil made his bigotry appear almost a mere eccentricity rather than the (literally) deadly serious matter that bigotry actually is.

I'm not saying that bigotry can never be a suitable subject for artistic or even humorous treatment, just that hatred is an extraordinarily difficult theme to transpose to an entertainment medium without risking damage to the social fabric of mutual tolerance and respect that is so precious to all of us—and so fragile.

One of the toughest test cases I've experienced is the humor of Sacha Baron Cohen, better known as Borat. Cohen is undoubtedly a brilliant young comedian, with a biting wit and an acting flair that make him compelling to watch. He is also a complex and interesting person—a Cambridge graduate (who acted in *Fiddler on the Roof* while in college), a practicing Jew from an Orthodox family, he has openly stated his desire to use his humor as a weapon to expose the ugliness of prejudice and, in particular, anti-Semitism.

I'm convinced that Cohen's intentions are excellent. But I'm not convinced that the comedic strategy he used in his megahit movie *Borat: Cultural Learnings of America for Make Benefit Glorious Nation of Kazakhstan* was entirely effective.

Consider what most people probably consider the most memorable scene in the picture—the one in which Borat teaches a collection of unsuspecting, real-life Americans in an Arizona bar the lyrics to what he claims is a traditional folk song from his homeland of Kazakhstan:

> *In my country there is problem*
> *And the problem is the Jew*
> *They take everybody money*
> *And they will not give back*
>
> [Chorus]
>
> *Throw the Jew down the well*
> *So the country can be free*
> *You must grab him by his horns*
> *And then we'll give a big party*

If you recall, the joke is that—after a long moment of shock—Borat's audience seems to happily join in the singing, enthusiastically shouting out, "Throw the Jew down the well!" as if nothing would please them more.

The scene certainly packs a punch—but, in retrospect, what does it tell us? That people in Arizona are secret bigots who are just waiting for a Borat to come along and encourage them to express it? I don't really believe that. That everyone has a little bit of prejudice deep inside that will come out in the right context? I already knew that.

The scene also leaves one feeling a bit queasy about Cohen's "ambush" filming technique, in which he tricked real people into appearing in the movie using a kind of *Candid Camera* approach. We're encouraged by the scene to conclude that the people in the bar are especially contemptible, possibly biased, maybe even evil—but is that really fair? Is it possible the Arizonans were simply torn between a variety of emotions—shock, confusion, distaste, and the desire not to embarrass or offend a supposed foreign visitor to our shores—and couldn't figure out an appropriate way of handling this bizarre situation? I think it is possible—and as a result I'm not convinced that the scene sheds any real light on what true bigotry is all about.

Other things about *Borat* bother me, too. I worry that the overall jolly, slapstick tone of the picture may have an effect *opposite* of the one Cohen apparently intends, making the ignorant bigot Borat appear a lovable, even sympathetic character. And, of course, the absurdly over-the-top caricature of the people of Kazakhstan as crude, filthy hillbillies is genuinely offensive. (And so unnecessary: Cohen could have easily made Borat a denizen of some mythical country without sacrificing any of the humor, such as it is.)

Then there is the edgy television cartoon series *South Park*, an equal-opportunity offender, which has repeatedly flirted with anti-Semitism through its Jewish character Kyle. In "Two Days Before the Day After Tomorrow," a typically surrealistic episode from the show's ninth season (first aired in October 2005), Kyle and another character, Cartman, are trapped in an apocalyptic nightmare that evidently has something to do with global warming. In the midst of this chaos, Cartman draws a gun and demands that Kyle give him his "Jew gold," a pouch of gold that every Jew supposedly hides on his person in case of emergency. This might seem like merely an over-the-top satire of anti-Semitic fantasies, except that it turns out that Kyle not only has a bag of Jew gold around his neck (which he throws away rather than allow Cartman to take it) but also a *decoy* bag that he carries specifically to fool the gentiles. Two stereotypes in one—not only are Jews obsessed with money, but they're crafty and deceptive as well!

As I say, *South Park* spares no one in its slash-and-burn comedy. The season eight episode "The Passion of the Jew" was an extreme satire of Mel Gibson's notorious film *The Passion of the Christ*, and was praised by the Jewish newspaper the *Forward* as "perhaps the most biting critique of 'The Passion' to date." When the ox that's gored by such over-the-top humor is that of someone such as Gibson, who at the very least plays carelessly with dangerous anti-Semitic stereotypes, I find myself sharing in the joke—and appreciating it.

But I still find the humor of *South Park* to be culturally risky. Although the producers emphasize, in their own defense, that the show is intended only for viewers over eighteen, I can't help suspecting that plenty of younger kids are watching it—and that many parents are lulled by the animated cartoon format into allowing them to tune in without appropriate supervision. And in any case, who says that everyone eighteen years or older is mature enough to understand the difference between laughing at bigotry and laughing with it?

It's important to note that ethnic stereotyping by Jewish comedians of *non-Jewish* people can be just as offensive as the use of anti-Semitic images. Thankfully, most Jewish comedians are pretty sensitive about the need to be respectful of people from every background, but there are some who, in their desire to push the envelope, have crossed the line into flirting with out-and-out bigotry. I'm thinking, for example, of the young comedian Sarah Silverman, whose stage persona as a naïve but prejudiced Jewish girl gives her license to use lines like "Of course the best time to get pregnant is when you're a black teenager"; radio talk show host Howard Stern, known for his "shock jock" act designed to offend practically everyone; and the veteran borscht-belt stand-up comic Jackie Mason, who in recent years has laced his routines with "social commentary" that includes disparaging remarks about African Americans and other ethnic groups.

Hey, guys—anti-Semitism isn't funny. And it's no better when we reverse the joke and direct the bigotry at others.

————

We need to keep this topic in perspective. I would never compare the stereotype-based humor of Jewish comedians, even when I disagree with it, to the truly hateful mockery and attacks disseminated every day on the Internet and in other venues by the anti-Semites of the world. The potential for psychological and social harm, plus the physical violence that those hatemongers incite, is far worse than any damage that a Borat might do. I certainly don't advocate censorship of movies, TV, or other forms of art in an attempt to purge them of ethnic stereotyping—that would be pointless, futile, and probably self-defeating in the long run.

What's more, we need to realize that there can be a fine line between insensitive stereotyping and artistic depictions of ethnic life that are genuinely uplifting, even educational. We mustn't be too hasty when condemning stereotypes in entertainment. Occasionally, stereotypes can be part of an artistic offering that, on balance, plays a positive role in fostering good community relations and understanding among peoples—not the reverse. Talent, sensitivity, and instincts seem to make the difference.

Some may worry that my unease with Jewish comedians making anti-Semitic stereotypes into the stuff of humor represents an inability to appreciate the power of laughter. Humor can indeed be a powerful weapon in the war against ignorance and intolerance. But it works not by simplistically reenacting or reinforcing hateful images of Jews. Just the opposite—it works by turning those stereotypes on their head in a creative way.

7

DAMNED IF WE DO, DAMNED IF WE DON'T

S tereotypes can be deadly. Over the past two millennia, the stereotypes about Jews have led, directly or indirectly, to a truly horrifying death toll. The countless, nameless Jews who were harassed, exiled, imprisoned, tortured, and killed for the crime of being heretics during the Middle Ages; the others who were burned as witches or murdered by mobs who blamed them for everything from bad harvests or unseasonable weather to an outbreak of the plague; the many who were killed in riots and pogroms whenever local economic or political conditions led to heightened communal tensions—all these were victims of the deadly power of bigotry. And that's without even including in the count the millions who perished when centuries of European anti-Semitism found their ultimate horrific expression in the Nazi Holocaust.

All of us, Jews and non-Jews alike, must never forget the power to kill that is embedded in stereotypes. But it's equally important to recognize the more insidious if subtle impact that stereotypes have on all of us, every day of our lives.

In contemporary America—thank goodness—anti-Semitism doesn't usually rise to the level of deadly hatred. It is, quite literally, a chronic sickness—one that doesn't kill us, but that we have to live with. And like most chronic illnesses, it has effects that go far beyond the obvious.

One of those effects is to blind large portions of society to realities that don't fit the myths enshrined in the stereotypes. In many cases, that blindness is merely an irritant. In other cases, it can be much more disabling, as eloquently described in a newspaper column titled "Jews Without Money" by Yonnasan Gershom. He wrote, in part:

> Many poor Jews are, quite frankly, afraid to admit that they are Jewish, for fear of being harassed or ridiculed. This is especially true in group homes, where acceptance by the other residents can make or break one's participation in the program. Paranoid? Perhaps. But I know the feeling, because I myself have had some unsettling encounters with stereotypes.
>
> For example, there was the bill collector who simply refused to believe that I was unemployed and had no cash on hand. He had apparently been informed that I was a rabbi, which, to him, meant that I must be drawing a fat salary from some suburban synagogue. (My ministry is mostly volunteer, supported over the years by a string of secular jobs.) At one point, this obnoxious man actually threatened to reveal my debts to my "congregation." My wife and I joked about that one for months, as we pictured this guy in a three-piece suit parading down Franklin Avenue with a sign proclaiming that Rabbi Gershom owed fifty dollars to the phone company!

Eventually I did find employment, which brought with it another set of Jewish stereotypes, beginning with the co-workers who openly wondered why a Jew would want such a low-paying job. (We get hungry, like everyone else.) Almost everyone told me stories about someone they knew who had worked for some rich Jew somewhere, oblivious to the fact that people who can afford to hire servants are, by definition, affluent—regardless or race, religion, or national origin.

To be a poor Jew is to be invisible; you do not become a statistic until you strike it rich. For ten years I lived in and around the Phillips neighborhood as a tenant, moving every couple years when the landlord raised the rent. As such, I was an anonymous part of the urban population. But when my wife and I finally managed to become home owners, we were miraculously transformed overnight into "Jewish Yuppies." All we had done was buy the same house we were renting, to avoid moving again. As Jews, we were seen as Yuppies; for any other minority, we would be "grass-roots people gaining control of our living space."

Gershom's account vividly illustrates the willful blindness of people who are so wedded to thinking in stereotypes that they aren't even aware of the limitations of their vision. Any slender piece of ev-idence that suggests a Jew is affluent—such as Gershom's ability, after many years, to scrape together the money to buy a house—is taken as confirming the accuracy of the stereotype that "all Jews have money." And all evidence to the contrary is either ignored (as it was by the bill collector who simply refused to acknowledge the to-him impossible notion of a financially challenged Jew) or, worse, becomes a pretext for actually mistreating the person who has had the effrontery to violate expectations (as with the group home residents who are harassed for being poor).

The human mind is an amazing thing. When it wants to cling to a fallacious belief in the face of overwhelming evidence to the contrary, it can find almost infinite ways of doing so—and all without any trace of self-awareness or self-questioning.

So bigotry has a powerful distorting effect on the lives of those who practice it. As Gershom observes, "To be a poor Jew is to be invisible." What must it be like to see humanity through a prism that renders millions of your fellow creatures invisible?—and not just poor Jews, of course, but also honest Jews, generous Jews, charitable Jews . . . to say nothing of intelligent and talented African Americans, hard-working Latinos, trustworthy Asians, and all the other myth-shattering people whose lives enrich the real world yet don't exist in the world of the bigot.

At the same time, of course, those who are on the receiving end of stereotyped attitudes also find their lives affected by the most pervasive myths about them—and not just in obvious ways, such as being subjected to insult, taunts, or attacks.

One of the sad effects of bigotry is the way the emotional, social, and political lives of Jews are distorted by the pervasiveness of Jewish stereotypes. Many Jews find themselves subtly altering their thinking and even their behavior specifically to avoid attracting attention to themselves—their economic status, their cultural characteristics, their "Jewishness." The result is a painful self-consciousness that makes it hard for many Jews just to live and be themselves, for fear of falling into one of the seemingly endless traps set for them by societal demands and expectations. Rabbi Gershom's reference to poor Jews who refuse to acknowledge their poverty—or to ask for the help they need—out of fear of arousing anti-Semitic hostility is one example. And there are other examples from other places on the social and economic ladder.

In American society, it's normal to take pride in one's business success, career achievements, and other accomplishments. People go out of their way to wear their Phi Beta Kappa keys, to mention their vacation homes, to allude to their kids at Ivy League colleges. All of this is pretty typical behavior and not objectionable so long as it's done in moderation and with taste.

Among many Jews, however, the same behavior is cause for endless agonizing. People wonder: If I mention that I just got a promotion at work, will my non-Jewish friends resent me as yet another social-climbing Jew—or wonder which of my co-religionists must have pulled strings behind the scenes to push my advancement? If I buy that high-end car, will I attract too much attention to myself among the neighbors on my block? If my daughter takes her nice new handbag to school tomorrow, will her classmates mark her down as a typical Jewish American Princess? Maybe it would be better to avoid problems by making different choices. But then wouldn't that be more phony than going ahead and doing what I want? What's the right answer?

It's a trick question, of course, because there is no "right answer."

This kind of anxiety is closely linked with the endless debating of "Is it good for the Jews?" that we alluded to in an earlier chapter. Among most ethnic groups, it's easy to figure out which circumstances are cause for celebration and which are cause for shame. When a Latina is named to the U.S. Supreme Court (Sonia Sotomayor), or a Chinese American wins a Grammy award (Yo-Yo Ma), or an Italian American becomes chairman of the Joint Chiefs of Staff (Peter Pace), fellow members of those ethnic groups simply rejoice. Why not? That's natural human behavior.

But when mainstream society has been attacking you for generations for what seems like "natural behavior," it's not so easy to respond that way. So Jews in America have long suffered anxiety attacks whenever one of their own becomes "too successful," "too visible," "too powerful." Marks of achievement, for Jews, are double-edged, attracting not just admiration and respect but also resentment, anger, and hostility.

Thus, when Connecticut Senator Joe Lieberman was named to the second spot on the national Democratic ticket in 2000, while many Jews celebrated, many others worried. Would gentiles who normally vote Democratic abandon the party? Would Lieberman say or do something on the campaign trail to stir up controversy and arouse anti-Semitism? Would the media portray Lieberman's religious beliefs and practices, or those of his family, in a caricatured or stereotyped way—and if they did, how should Jews as a whole respond? If the Gore-Lieberman ticket lost the election, would other Democrats blame "the Jew" and vow never again to nominate one of his faith? Or if they won, would the bigots use the result as further evidence that "Jews own this country" and "Jewish money decides elections"?

In the event, none of the dire consequences many Jews worried about came to pass. Extreme bigots, of course, were hostile to Lieberman. But the mainstream media and the vast mass of voters treated him and his religion with respect. And when the 2000 election ended up being decided by a controversial Supreme Court ruling about hanging chads in Florida, the religious heritage of the losing vice presidential candidate quickly disappeared as a factor in most people's minds.

But the benign result (for the Jews) of the Lieberman candidacy didn't end the sense of anxiety among Jewish people over any notable news event involving Jews. We've seen all too often how even events that have literally nothing to do with Jews can be twisted into blame-the-Jews extravaganzas, as when anti-Semites blamed the 9/11 attacks on (of all the unlikely theories) a Jewish conspiracy.

So we can't help asking about everything on the news, "Is it good for the Jews?" And since the underground stream of hostility toward the Jews seems never-ending, it's almost impossible to imagine any event involving prominent Jews that is an unmixed blessing. Absolutely *anything* is sufficient to arouse the hatred of a born hater—and deep inside, that's what many anti-Semitic bigots are.

The somewhat perverse emotional effects on Jews of this kind of hostile environment are illustrated amusingly by an article in *New York* magazine by journalist Jennifer Senior, written in response to the supposed discovery by scientists of a gene that makes Jews smarter than other people. (Hey, I didn't make this up—I'm just reporting what I read.) Senior recalls having had, for years, a list in her head of the great Jewish figures she was proud to be associated with: "Freud and Marx, Einstein and Bohr, Mendelssohn and Mahler. The brothers Gershwin. The brothers Marx. Woody Allen. Bob Dylan. Franz Kafka. Claude Lévi-Strauss. Bobby Fischer." She used to enjoy supplementing her list with names from Jewhoo, a Web site (now defunct) that was devoted to listing and honoring notable Jewish achievers. So imagine her dismay when she discovered, while surfing the Internet one day, that virtually the same list, under the heading *Jewish Controlled Entertainment,* was posted on jewwatch.com, a notorious hate site.

The irony is overwhelming: The very same facts that make Jews proud of their identity are, for bigots, an additional cause to fear and despise the Jews! No wonder Woody Allen portrays his archetypal Jewish *nebbish* character as a bundle of nerves and neuroses—you would be, too, if you found that literally *everything* about you could be construed as a reason to hate you.

Senior goes on to say:

> Personally, I'm always struck by how many Jews confess to a certain ambivalence about the volume and visibility of their accomplishments, as if there were something slightly vulgar or shameful about them. The friend who introduced me to Jewhoo confided that a friend of his, also Jewish, kept a list of Jews he wished were not. I realized I kept the same mental list. (Andy Fastow, the crook from Enron, is currently No. 1.)

Probably Bernie Madoff has now supplanted Andy Fastow on Senior's second list.

This sense of ambiguity—of Jews somehow feeling ashamed about the same things that logically should be a source of pride—connects neatly to one of the big problems about having to live with biased stereotypes: the fact that there is no way of behaving that can ever "disprove" them.

You can play this one almost like a game—but one with no way to win. Should affluent Jews give openly to charity? Then they are "flaunting their wealth." Should they give anonymously? Then they are "conspiring to hide their wealth." Should they give to Jewish causes? Then they are "keeping the wealth to themselves." Should they give to non-Jewish causes? Then they are "using their wealth to push in where they don't belong." Should their lifestyle reflect their affluence? Then they are being "crass and ostentatious." Should they bend over backwards to live simply and plainly? Then they are being "cheap and miserly."

In short, you're damned if you do, damned if you don't.

The conundrum of "damned if you do, damned if you don't" reflects more than just the irrationality of bigotry. It also reflects the ambiguity of attitudes toward money among Americans and in modern Western societies generally.

The truth is that most people don't quite know how they feel about money.

On the one hand, we all need it to survive, and we all like the things we can buy with it. So naturally we all like and want money, at least to some extent. In the United States, in particular, we seem to value wealth quite highly—after all, when given a choice, Americans often choose to work harder and longer than people in other countries in order to enjoy greater financial rewards, rather than dialing down our work efforts and experiencing greater leisure in exchange for less money. (Hence the term often used to describe the United States—a "consumption economy," driven by ever-growing consumer demand.) We often lionize wealthy people, as evidenced by countless television shows, magazine articles, and books devoted to chronicling their privileged lifestyles and promoting their wisdom.

Yet a part of us feels ambivalent about our desire for money. We use expressions like "filthy lucre," repeat old sayings like "The love of money is the root of all evil," and decry the influence of money in fields ranging from politics to sports. We make fun of people who pursue money too aggressively and overtly, and we take pleasure in the downfall of people who shamelessly flaunt their wealth, from flamboyant tycoons like Dennis Kozlowski to jet-setting heiresses like Paris Hilton.

Our society's ambiguous feelings about money and wealth are clearly reflected in its ambiguous attitudes toward successful Jews. Many non-Jews profess to admire Jews who have achieved economic success. But often not far below the surface is an undercurrent of envy. No less a cultural icon than America's greatest humorist, Mark Twain, even attributed the bulk of European anti-Semitism to this envy: "I am persuaded," he wrote in his 1898 essay "Concerning the Jews," "that in Russia, Austria, and Germany nine-tenths of the hostility to the Jew comes from the average Christian's inability to compete successfully with the average Jew in business."

As we've seen, Twain's observation that Jews were in the nineteenth century consistently more successful in business than non-Jews wasn't strictly true then, and it doesn't hold today. But there is this core of truth in his observation: If non-Jews come to accept the equation "Successful Capitalist = Jew," then the attitude of the non-Jew toward the Jew will reflect all the ambiguities of his attitude toward wealthy people in general. So the image of the Jew becomes a lightning rod attracting all the varied emotions people feel about money, wealth, and the power that goes with it.

Twain himself exhibited this ambiguity quite vividly a little later in the same essay I just quoted ("Concerning the Jews"). Speaking of Theodor Herzl, the pioneering Zionist leader, Twain wrote:

> Have you heard of his plan? He wishes to gather the Jews of the world together in Palestine, with a government of their own—under the suzerainty of the Sultan, I suppose. At the convention of Berne last year [1897], there were delegates from everywhere, and the proposal was received with decided favor. I am not the Sultan, and I am not objecting; but if that concentration of the cunningest brains in the world was going to be made in a free country (bar Scotland), I think it would be politic to stop it. It will not be well to let that race find out its strength. If the horses knew theirs, we should not rise any more.

I suppose referring to the Jews as "the cunningest brains in the world" might be construed as a compliment—but comparing us to horses? I'm sure Twain would say he was writing with tongue in cheek. Yet stereotypes are still stereotypes, and they rankle.

In her book *In Cheap We Trust: The Story of a Misunderstood American Virtue*, journalist Lauren Weber effectively captured the ambiguity of our attitude toward money:

> For many immigrants, extreme frugality (often coupled with extreme poverty) was the path not to Revolutionary-era yeoman independence, but to the kind of conspicuous consumption that the United States has come to represent. Immigrants (Jews, Chinese, and others) usually don't scrimp and save in order to have a simple cottage in the woods; they do it to have a big house on a fancy block (or to send their kids to Ivy League schools so *they* can ultimately have a big house on a fancy block). Like the rest of their adopted countrymen, they are caught in the American yo-yo swing between frugality and extravagance. And yet, trapped inside multiple and sometimes contradictory stereotypes, they cannot always spend their way to membership in the mainstream of American society.

It's not so unusual that a society should express its ambiguous feelings about cultural and moral values by singling out a minority to serve as a vessel for the related anxieties and aggressions. We see something similar in the realm of sexual mores, in which most Americans profess a faith in family values that include strict adherence to heterosexual monogamy even as they revel (often secretly) in the freedoms provided by our hypersexualized twenty-first-century society. The way some people and groups deal with the intense inner conflict this creates is by singling out some minority—"the gays," for example—to symbolize the dangers and immoralities they fear. When it comes to Americans' conflicted feelings about money, the Jews are often the preferred target group.

As Mark Twain pointed out, mixed feelings about wealth also shade easily into simple envy of those who are more successful than we are—an envy that easily turns poisonous when "those others" are perceived as "less deserving" than "our people." In his recent book *Capitalism and the Jews,* historian Jerry Z. Muller observes:

> [Economist] Joseph Schumpeter regarded resentment as the almost inevitable by-product of the dynamism that is characteristic of capitalism; and [economist] Friedrich Hayek noted that it was the Jews who were often made to bear the brunt of such resentment. That resentment came not only from the lower classes, but from the members of the erstwhile upper classes when they found themselves losing their relative social status as new money displaced old. For old money, the makers of new money are by definition pushy and aggressive parvenus.

"Pushy and aggressive"—it's easy to hear the voice of anti-Semitic prejudice creeping into that all-too-common description of successful Jews. It's language we often hear from people who, under normal circumstances, tend to admire those who have achieved wealth through their own efforts. The rules, apparently, are different when the hero (or heroine) of the entrepreneurial success story is Jewish. Muller goes on to quote commentator Thomas Sowell, who, as a noted African American conservative, is no stranger to the social and psychological tensions that exist between minority groups and mainstream society:

> While some observers might regard [the] determination and resourcefulness [of successful minority group members] as admirable or inspiring, to others the rise of middleman minorities from poverty to prosperity has been like a slap across the face. If accepted as an achievement, it raises painful questions about others who have achieved nothing comparable, despite in some cases being initially more fortunate. Someone who was born rich represents no such assault on the ego and creates no such resentment or hostility. Anyone who can offer an alternative explanation of these middlemen's success—such as calling them "parasites" or "bloodsuckers" who have prospered at the expense of others—has been popular in many countries and some have built entire careers and whole movements on such popularity. When people are presented with the alternatives of hating themselves for their failure or hating others for their success, they seldom choose to hate themselves.

Sowell's last observation is dead-on, of course: Much bigotry is driven by insecurity, self-doubt, and shame. It's so much easier to turn those emotions outward and make them the vehicle for attacking a supposed enemy rather than grappling honestly with their painful implications.

If you wonder whether tensions between Christians and Jews—and often within Jews themselves—are really connected with our ambiguous attitudes toward money itself, consider a recent article in *Jewish World Review* that happened to be provoked by the author's disagreement with my own organization, the ADL.

Titled "Jews and Money: When Anti-Semitism Isn't," the article by Rabbi Avi Shafran took issue with the ADL about a situation I mentioned earlier in this book—when two South Carolina Republican party leaders tried to praise Senator Jim DeMint, a fiscal conservative, by comparing him to financially successful Jews who "got that way not by watching dollars, but instead by taking care of the pennies and the dollars taking care of themselves." In Rabbi Shafran's view, ADL's southeast regional director overreacted to this ethnic stereotyping when he said that the politicians' retraction of the statement wasn't sufficient. "Harping on a hapless comment after a clear apology," Shafran remarked, "does seem somewhat puzzling."

I'm not interested in reopening a debate on this fairly minor (though revealing) incident. What does interest me, however, is what Rabbi Shafran went on to say about the entire controversy:

> More puzzling, however—at least to me—was the umbrage-taking in the first place. Why is imputing fiscal responsibility to successful Jews offensive? It isn't as if the South Carolinians insinuated that such Jews are dishonest or even miserly. They simply attributed to us Hebrews—at least the materially successful among us—a keen awareness

of the fact that even a small thing has value. When exactly did frugality became bad?

My guess is that it was around the time the wildly wasteful consumer culture all around us took hold, when people began to make "living in the moment" (or, less charitably put, "ignoring the future") a high ideal. But whatever the origin of its abandonment, the idea that everything has worth is not shameful. In fact, it's thoroughly Jewish. As the Talmud puts it, "Each and every penny contributes to a large sum" (*Bava Basra,* 9b).

In one sense, the rabbi is completely right. There's certainly nothing shameful or despicable about frugality. Being a good steward of whatever wealth God has seen fit to bless you with is consistent with being a good steward of creation as a whole; wasting money is just one step away from being wasteful of our world's natural resources, the environment, and the labor others have contributed to our own good fortune. Jews *should* be careful with money, their own and others—and they should be proud of it. We can all wish Bernie Madoff had learned this lesson a little better!

And yet, for the rabbi to be "puzzled" at the offense I and many other Jews felt over the politicians' remark seems just a bit disingenuous. It's true that, in itself, the stereotype being invoked is not demeaning. But when it comes to Jews, money, and the attitudes of the gentiles, nothing exists "in itself." Everything takes place in the context of a two-thousand-year-old tradition of mistrust, suspicion, intolerance, and even hatred. In that context, we've all seen, far too often, the concept of frugality shading easily and imperceptibly into "stinginess" and then into "avarice" and "dishonesty."

No wonder we react as if our buttons have been pushed when someone "compliments" us on our frugality. We've lost count of the number of times when someone used a back-handed compliment just like this as a way of putting us Jews in our place—a smile proving to be practically indistinguishable from a sneer. You know the kind of compliment I mean: "Oh, you Jews are so clever in business!" "If you want to make sure your tax return gives you every advantage—and I mean *every possible* advantage—hire a Jewish accountant!" "I knew I'd never get the better of that deal—I was negotiating with a Jew!"

With compliments like these, who needs insults?

Once again, the double bind of bigotry catches us in its snare. If we say nothing when we're on the receiving end of double-edged compliments like these, we may seem to be acknowledging the correctness of the stereotypes they embody, and maybe even the correctness of all the slimy implications that go with them. But if we respond by pointing out the offensive nature of all stereotyping as well as the sinister link between the "compliment" and the vicious accusations Jews have endured for centuries, then we're "overreacting," being "touchy," demonstrating that Jews "have no sense of humor," and maybe even exposing yet again the excessive pride (dare I say megalomania?) of "God's chosen people."

Of course, my disagreement with Rabbi Shafran doesn't mean that I think the rabbi is in any way intolerant or biased against his own people! My point is that the weirdly ambiguous position in which Jews find themselves because of the history of hatred we must constantly live with makes almost *any* response on our part feel awkward and uncomfortable—and is quite likely to be used against us by those who have hatred in their hearts. Damned if we do, damned if we don't.

Further complicating this sense of ambiguity are the subtle but important differences between Christian and Jewish attitudes toward wealth.

In truth, there are many commonalities between the money-related values that Christians have and those that Jews have. That's only natural, since the two faiths grow from the same historical roots, worship the same God, and share many of the same stories, scriptures, and heroes. In both religions, the Earth and all its riches are created and blessed by God. In both, human beings are charged with protecting, nurturing, and improving that bounty through wise stewardship. In both, humans are absolutely required to share their wealth, however great or small, with those who are less fortunate. All these values are prominently illustrated throughout both the Hebrew Scriptures and the Christian New Testament, and most people of both religions are happy to endorse them jointly.

But there are differences, too, many of which grow out of the historical development of the two faiths.

Christianity has a strong tinge of asceticism—a belief in the value of physical and sensual self-denial, deprivation, even suffering. This attitude is so powerful that theologians say it sometimes borders on Manicheanism—the suspicion that the physical world and everything in it, including human beings, is unavoidably tinged with evil. No mainstream Christian church actually subscribes to Manicheanism, which the Roman Catholic church (among others) has long considered heretical. But the influence of Manicheanism can be seen in many threads of Christian belief, practice, behavior, and attitudes: for example, in the asceticism of monastic life; in the stress laid on practices of self-denial during penitential seasons like Lent; and in the importance assigned by many Christians and Christian groups to sexual purity (which often means, in practice, sexual abstinence).

These beliefs and practices don't have any real counterparts in mainstream Judaism. By and large, Jews believe that the world and all that is in it is good, and that God wants us to enjoy it fully. In his marvelous *Book of Jewish Values: A Day-by-Day Guide to Ethical Living*, Rabbi Joseph Telushkin has summed up this attitude extremely well:

> Judaism believes that the pursuit of pleasure, if done in moderation, is good. The Talmud teaches, "In the future world, a man will have to give an accounting for every good thing his

eyes saw, but of which he did not eat" (Palestinian Talmud, *Kiddushin* 4:12). It relates that Rabbi Elazar "paid particular attention to this statement, setting aside money so that he could eat every kind of food at least once a year." . . . And while individual Jewish scholars have lived and encouraged lives of asceticism, the more normative Jewish view is that taught by Maimonides: "No one should, by vows and oaths, forbid to himself the use of things otherwise permitted" (*Mishneh Torah*, "Laws of Character Development," 3:1).

This belief in the goodness of enjoying life to the fullest gives Judaism a quality of exuberance and joy that Jews find deeply nurturing and that many non-Jews find highly attractive. But it also causes some suspicion among non-Jews. If you were raised to associate being religious with self-deprivation, suffering, and looking gloomy, and if you think dancing, singing, and eating and drinking fine foods are self-indulgences that God is likely to frown upon, then you may find the Jewish way of living and worshiping God to be frivolous, if not downright sinful. You might call this a theological difference between Christians and Jews, but I think it's really a cultural difference—a set of subtle, largely unconscious attitudes that each group has developed over time that may lead to misunderstandings and even hostility between us. I suspect that some of the bad feelings that some Christians harbor toward Jews in relation to wealth may be traceable to this cultural divide. For example, it may make a lavish bar mitzvah or bat mitzvah, which many Jews consider a simple expression of joy shared with friends and family, appear irreligious, flashy, or hypocritical to a Christian onlooker.

It would be easy to overstate these differences. In reality, there's a lot of overlap between Christian and Jewish attitudes toward wealth, especially in a country like the United States where we participate together in a culture that reflects both faiths as well as many other influences. The challenges concerning how we choose to express our personal and religious values in everyday life decisions affect people of every background and creed, not just Jews. Nonetheless, differences in Jewish and non-Jewish cultural attitudes do play a role in fostering stereotyped images of one another—particularly among people who don't really know members of the other group and are willing to think negative thoughts about them precisely because they are the "other."

Of course, not all Christians think and feel the same way about material wealth and its uses, nor do all Jews. There's a significant movement among Jews today, for example, to scale back the amount of money and other resources that are spent on bar mitzvah and bat mitzvah celebrations in favor of more modest, economically sustainable, and environmentally friendly practices. The current economic downturn certainly encourages this trend. And Mazon, the Jewish charity dedicated to alleviating hunger among people of all religions and ethnic backgrounds, is one of many groups that urge socially conscious Jews to donate a percentage of what they spend on bar and bat mitzvahs or on wedding parties to help the poor—a response to human need that is very much in the mainstream of Jewish tradition.

The tension between social pressure to spend lavishly on family events and the desire to use financial resources in more modest ways that may produce greater long-term value is not brand new. The same conflict existed in ancient Israel, as a passage about funeral services from the Babylonian Talmud cited by Rabbi Telushkin reminds us:

> Formerly, they used to bring food to the house of mourning, rich people in baskets of silver and gold, poor people in baskets of peeled willow twigs; and the poor felt ashamed. Therefore a law was passed that everybody should bring food in baskets of willow twigs, in deference to the poor. . . . Formerly, they used to serve drinks in a house of mourning, the rich serving in white glasses and the poor in colored glasses [which were less expensive]; and the poor felt ashamed. Therefore a law was passed that everyone should serve drinks in colored glasses, in deference to the poor . . . (*Mo'ed Kattan*, 27a).

This Talmudic passage shows that respect for the sensibilities of people of modest means and a desire to avoid overly lavish displays of wealth have been part of Jewish values for centuries. Yet even here the damned-if-you-do, damned-if-you-don't dilemma may raise its ugly head. The Jewish family that spends a large sum on a social occasion may well be criticized as "crass," "showy," and "having no class" by people who have been infected with stereotyped beliefs about Jews. But their neighbors who choose to spend less (perhaps quietly donating the difference to charity) may be subject to just as much criticism on the grounds of being cheap, stingy, and grasping—which, of course, is simply a different set of anti-Jewish stereotypes. The rules are the same: Heads I win, tails you lose.

Only one rational conclusion is possible in the face of such determined irrationality. Since there is no way that Jewish behavior can be tailored to escape the condemnation of bigots, Jews simply have to try to live good lives according to their best values and beliefs, without being defensive or reactive—even though this is never easy.

In a perfect world, all of God's creatures would be able to appreciate themselves and one another for the interesting, varied, and infinitely valuable beings their creator shaped them to be. We may never achieve such a world here on Earth. But if we want to get a little closer, a good way to start would be to rid ourselves and our society of the corrosive effect of stereotypes. Believing lies about one another does no one any good; all it does is create different classes of victims.

EPILOGUE

The subject of anti-Semitism is not a pleasant one, and some of the examples of bigotry and intolerance I've shared with you reflect human nature at its worst. Yet the majority of American people truly care about helping our country live up to its noblest ideals.

What can we all do, as Americans, to combat the evil effects of stereotyping, prejudice, and hatred, and in particular the use of discredited beliefs about Jews and money?

My lifetime spent on the front lines of the battle for respect and understanding has taught me that there are many things that ordinary citizens can and should do to combat intolerance in our own homes, communities, workplaces, and religious institutions.

Perhaps the simplest and most important is education—developing and sharing knowledge and information about bigotry. It's a crucial activity for every well-meaning citizen to participate in. I think it's important for every concerned citizen to make it his or her business to stay informed on a regular basis about the problems of extremism and intolerance.

That means that you shouldn't turn a blind eye when the problem of bigotry pops up on your radar screen, nor should you shy away from letting other people know what you learn about the causes and manifestations of intergroup hatred.

If you turn on a TV news panel and hear one or more of the commentators uttering remarks that sound biased—about Jewish financial power, let's say—don't just change the station or fume silently and ineffectually. Take a few minutes to check the facts behind the myths—used with judgment and discretion, the Internet is a powerful tool for this—and then send an e-mail or make a phone call to the station to express your views. You may be surprised to find how powerful a few forceful complaints from ordinary citizens can be.

Similarly, if you see a letter to the editor in your local newspaper or a comment on your favorite Internet site that mindlessly repeats a vicious stereotype, don't just ignore it. Arm yourself with information to refute the lie and then lift your voice in protest by writing a letter or comment of your own.

Make yourself into an informed citizen about the dangers of extremism and bigotry, and become a beacon of knowledge and reason in whatever circles you frequent.

The self-education process, however, goes beyond reading about intolerance in others. It also includes the much more challenging process of probing the deep-seated causes of intolerance in the psyche of the person you know best—yourself.

Much as we'd like to deny it, there are traces of bias in all of us. It's almost inevitable, given that we've all been raised in a society in which stereotypes are everywhere—in newspapers, books, movies, and on television, in folk culture, and in the common sayings and assumptions that fill daily conversation. Enlightened and tolerant as you may be, there are probably, just a little below the surface, some attitudes and feelings inside you that you wouldn't be proud for the world to see.

Ask yourself, "Is there anything I can do to overcome the uncomfortable feeling I have about *that* kind of person?" In many cases, just being aware of your own tiny trace of prejudice is enough to disinfect it and keep it from growing to dangerous proportions.

Look inside yourself with curiosity and candor, and you may discover that prejudice isn't just a problem for somebody *else* to deal with.

———

Having taken seriously the responsibility we all have to educate ourselves about intolerance, there is a further, extremely crucial educational role played by all adults who have a connection of any sort with a child. Most learning goes on outside the classroom, and when it comes to an issue like intolerance, that is doubly true. Whether you are a parent or grandparent, an aunt or uncle, a schoolteacher or scout leader, a youth leader in a local temple, synagogue, church, or mosque, or just an average person whose life brushes up against the lives of young people, you have a powerful opportunity to teach—through words, actions, and attitudes—the value of respecting every human being and of standing up against hatred in every form.

As adults, we are leaders for all the young people around us. We owe it to them not to ignore any budding seeds of racism, ethnocentrism, sexism, or any other form of prejudice, but to take them seriously and do everything we can to try to help the next generation grow up freer from the infection of intolerance.

———

We also each have a role to play in making sure that our communities stand squarely against bigotry in any form.

We're each a part of many communities. The neighborhood where you live, the office where you work, the clubs and associations you're a member of, the house of worship you attend—these are just a few of the communities you belong to and where your words and actions have an impact.

Standing up against bigotry on a daily basis is very important, even when the problems of prejudice are seemingly small, subtle, and easy to ignore. With small, courageous acts, there's a chance we can move our communities in the direction of being truly free of prejudice.

Another way you can play a role in combating bigotry is by working to improve the atmosphere of civility and mutual respect surrounding political debate.

When you participate in vigorous give-and-take, it is a wonderful hallmark of American society. And, of course, when political arguments begin to slide toward anti-Semitism or other forms of prejudice—when ancient ugly stereotypes such as those about Jews and money rear their heads in place of reasoned debate, and when threats, name-calling, and finger-pointing seem to make constructive dialogue impossible—I hope yours will be one of the voices calling for calm, reason, and mutual respect. All three are qualities we could surely use more of in our national conversation.

The ADL also regards as an important part of its mission the defense of religious freedom. We consider the separation of church and state essential to preserving religious freedom in our increasingly pluralistic society.

Finally, it's important that all Americans be firmly committed to opposing bigotry and hatred no matter what group is being victimized. Although the ADL is a Jewish organization, and proud of it, we stand with anyone who is the target of physical, verbal, or mental attacks, and seek to defend the rights of all people to live in peace, freedom, and mutual respect.

This is a value most Americans would be proud to claim as their own—yet it's a very difficult one to live up to in practice. We all have that grain of tribal loyalty inside us that makes us care just a little more about "people like us" than about "those others." Maybe it has evolutionary roots: There may have been an adaptive value to behaviors that increased the survival rate of "my" genes as opposed to those of the people in the next valley. But whatever the cause, we all have this tendency, and in most cases it does no harm. It's usually expressed in such forms as our love for a culture and traditions we find familiar and beautiful, the pride we feel about accomplishments by members of our group, and the desire to see what is best about our heritage preserved and extended into future generations.

The problem arises when we take this attitude toward the negative side—when we fail to recognize that the culture, traditions, accomplishments, and heritage of *other* groups are equally valuable.

Such recognition is the crucial corrective to ethnic pride and loyalty, and we must never lose sight of it.

I think that one of the corollaries of this truth is that we must each make a special effort to challenge our own assumptions and prejudices. This requires imagination. It means trying to see situations through the eyes of someone with a very different background from yours. It means empathizing with the difficulties they've faced, the prejudices they've had to battle against, and the impediments to success they've had to overcome. And it means resisting the lure of zero-sum thinking—the assumption that a win for "those other people" must mean a loss for me and mine. In pluralistic America, we can *all* rise together. In fact, we must.

Maybe the *worst* lesson anyone could take away from this book is the idea that vigorously opposing anti-Semitism means somehow being against gentiles. Substituting one form of prejudice for another would get us nowhere. Let's not go that route.

To return to one of the first points I made in this book, anti-Semitism is, unfortunately, not a history lesson—it's a current event. But that's not an unmitigated tragedy. It means we all have the opportunity, in our daily lives, to lend our strength to the ongoing battle to make our world a more tolerant, open-minded, and freedom-loving place. If we can do this, we'll leave our children a better planet than the one we inherited. Let's resolve to make this not just a pleasant dream, but a living reality.

ACKNOWLEDGEMENTS

The subject of this book has always been on my mind. The need to write crystallized for me as I watched the world overtaken by an economic meltdown. The age-old anti-Semitic canards about Jews and money, while never completely absent, suddenly re-emerged with a vengeance and I was compelled to metaphorically take pen to paper.

To those who helped me through this project I say thank you.

I am especially indebted to Karl Weber, for his ability to grasp my thoughts on the subject in a serious and cogent way. His patience and guidance resulted in translating my ideas into this book. He is my literary partner and friend.

Thank you to my agent, Lynne Rabinoff, for her support, enthusiasm and commitment.

My publisher Airié Stuart of Palgrave Macmillan never wavered in her belief in the importance of this undertaking, for which I am most appreciative.

I am grateful to the Anti-Defamation League's current National Chair, Robert G. Sugarman, and past Chair, Glen S. Lewy, for their support and understanding.

A special thank you to my ADL colleagues who provided their expertise: our Civil Rights staff for their thorough research; Ken Jacobson, for his extraordinary insight and wise counsel; and Myrna Shinbaum, who kept me on track and shepherded the project through to its fruition.

LIST OF SOURCES

This book is not a work of original scholarship. Experts in the history of Judaism and anti-Semitism will recognize that I've relied on the research of others who have devoted lifetimes to studying these topics. This includes the research staff of the Anti-Defamation League, for whose work I am deeply grateful. The list of sources below, keyed to topics discussed in the book, is provided so that the curious reader can review the specific books and articles I've drawn details from and, if desired, read more deeply in the works I've found useful and interesting.—*A.F.*

CHAPTER 1. THE BERNIE MADOFF MOMENT

Sources for the Aaron Feuerstein story: "Malden Mills Industries, Inc—Company History." Funding Universe. Online at http://www .fundinguniverse.com/company-histories/Malden-Mills-Industries-Inc-Company-History.html. "The Mensch of Malden Mills," by

Rebecca Leung. CBS News, July 6, 2003. Online at http://www.cbs news.com/stories/2003/07/03/60minutes/main561656.shtml. "The Glow from a Fire," by Steve Wulf. *Time,* Jan. 8, 1996. Online at http://www.time.com/time/magazine/article/0,9171,983916,00 .html. "Malden Mills owner applies religious ethics to business," by Kenneth D. Campbell. *MIT Tech Talk,* April 16, 1997. Online at http://web.mit.edu/newsoffice/1997/mills–0416.html. "Fabled Mill Owner Works to Manufacture a Miracle," by Jeffrey Klineman. *Forward,* July 25, 2003. Online at http://www.forward.com.articles/ 7736/. "Malden Mills survives another kind of fire." *Boston Globe,* Aug. 15, 2003. Online at http://articles.baltimoresun.com/2003-08-15/business/0308150283_1_feuerstein-malden-mills-unsecured-creditors. "Altruism? Bah, Humbug," by Radley Balko. *Apple Daily,* Dec. 22, 2004. Online at Cato Institute Web site at http://www .cato.org/pub_display.php?pub_id=2923.

Sources for the Bernie Madoff story: "Standing Accused: A Pillar of Finance and Charity," by Alan Feuer and Christine Haughney. *New York Times,* Dec. 13, 2008. Online at http://www.nytimes.com/ 2008/12/13/nyregion/13madoff.html. "Why It Matters That Madoff Is Jewish: Journalist J. J. Goldberg on Jews and the Money Culture," by Josh Nathan-Kazis. *Newvoices,* May 18, 2009. Online at http:// www.newvoices.org/community?id=0011. "Madoff Wall Street fraud threatens Jewish philanthropy," by Gabrielle Birkner and Anthony Weiss. *Haaretz*.com, Dec. 14, 2008. Online at http://www

.haaretz.com/hasen/spages/1046187.html. "The Talented Mr. Mad-off," by Julie Creswell and Landon Thomas Jr. *New York Times,* Jan. 25, 2009. Online at http://www.nytimes.com/2009/01/25/business/ 25bernie.html. "Anti-Semitism and the Madoff Scandal." Anti-Defamation League, Dec. 19, 2008. Online at http://www.adl.org/ main_Anti_Semitism_Domestic/Anti-Semitism+and+the+Ma-doff+Scandal.htm. "Bernard Madoff and the Jews of Palm Beach," by Laurence Leamer. *Huffington Post,* Dec. 12, 2008. Online at http:// www.huffingtonpost.com/laurence-leamer/bernard-madoff-and-the-sh_b_150624.html. "Bernard Madoff, Bad for the Jews," by Richard Silverstein. *The Guardian* (U.K.), Dec. 23, 2008. Online at http://www.guardian.co.uk/commentisfree/cifamerica/2008/dec/23/ bernard-madoff-jewish-charities. "The Top Ten Craziest Things Ever Said During a U.N. Speech," by Joshua Keating. *Foreign Policy,* Sept. 25, 2009. Online at http://www.foreignpolicy.com/articles/ 2009/09/24/the_top_10_craziest_things_ever_said_during_a_un _speech?page=full. "Fraud Case Shakes a Billionaire's Caribbean Realm," by Clifford Krause, Julie Creswell, and Charlie Savage. *New York Times,* Feb. 21, 2009. Online at http://www.nytimes.com/2009/ 02/21/business/21stanford.html.

Anti-Semitic comments in response to the 2008–2009 financial crisis: See "Financial Crisis Sparks Wave of Internet Anti-Semitism." Anti-Defamation League, Oct. 2, 2008. Online at http://www.adl .org/main_internet/Anti-Semitism_Financial_Crisis.htm.

CHAPTER 2. THE STORY OF A STEREOTYPE

"Scholars like the late James Parkes": See, for example, his books *The Conflict of the Church and Synagogue: a Study in the Origins of Anti-Semitism* (London: Soncino Press, 1934); *End of an Exile: Israel, the Jews and the Gentile World* (London: Vallentine, Mitchell, 1954); *A History of the Jewish People* (London: Weidenfeld and Nicolson, 1962); and *Antisemitism* (London: Vallentine, Mitchell, 1963).

"Reinforcing these legal restrictions was what scholar George M. Frederickson has described as 'a folk mythology'": *Racism: A Short History,* by George M. Frederickson (Princeton, NJ: Princeton University Press, 2002), p. 20.

Treatment of Jews in Medieval Muslim world: *Sea of Faith: Islam and Christianity in the Medieval Mediterranean World,* by Stephen O'Shea (New York: Walker, 2006).

"In the words of Heinrich Heine": *The Memoirs of Heinrich Heine,* 1884.

"We see this link in its most extreme form in terrorist Osama bin Laden's 'Letter to America'": Printed in *The Observer* (United Kingdom), Nov. 24, 2002. Online at http://www.guardian.co.uk/world/2002/nov/24/theobserver.

"As historian H. H. Ben-Sasson has suggested": Quoted in *Antisemitism: Myth and Hate from Antiquity to the Present,* by Marvin

Perry and Frederick M. Schweitzer (London: Palgrave Macmillan, 2002), p. 125.

"And as one chronicler of the period, Jacob von Königshofen of Strasbourg, recorded": Quoted in *Antisemitic Myths: A Historical and Contemporary Anthology,* edited by Marvin Perry and Frederick M. Schweitzer (Bloomington: Indiana University Press, 2008), pp. 27–28.

"Historian Benzion Netanyahu": *The Origins of the Inquisition in Fifteenth Century Spain,* by B. Netanyahu (New York: New York Review Books, 2001, 2nd ed.).

"Karl Marx, father of socialism, saw the Jews": Karl Marx quotations from "The Jewish Question," 1843; quoted in *Antisemitic Myths,* pp. 79–81.

"Decades later, though writing from a very different perspective, and with admiration, economist John Maynard Keynes depicted": Quoted in *Capitalism and the Jews,* by Jerry Z. Muller (Princeton, NJ: Princeton University Press, 2010), p. 63.

Anti-Semitism of Henry Ford: *Henry Ford and the Jews: The Mass Production of Hate,* by Neil Baldwin (New York: Public Affairs, 2001).

"In response, the German military high command": Discussed in *The Pity of It All,* by Amos Elon (New York: Metropolitan Books, 2002), p. 338.

"This is one of the central themes of the infamous czarist-era forgery, *The Protocols of the Learned Elders of Zion*" Quoted in *Antisemitic Myths,* p. 142.

"The survival of this fantasy into our own day": Pat Robertson quote from *The Religious Right: The Assault on Tolerance and Pluralism in America* (New York: Anti-Defamation League, 1994).

"As historian Jerry Z. Muller writes": *Capitalism and the Jews*, p. 31.

"In her book *In Cheap We Trust*, Lauren Weber": *In Cheap We Trust: The Story of a Misunderstood American Virtue*, by Lauren Weber (New York: Little, Brown, 2009), p. 100.

"I'm thinking, for example, of the students at Cornell University": "Education: Bigots in the Ivory Tower," by Nancy Gibbs. *Time*, May 7, 1990. Online at http://www.time.com/time/magazine/article/0,9171,970015,00.html.

"Essayist Daniel L. Alexander has described his personal encounter": "The Japanese and the Jews," by Daniel L. Alexander, *First Things*, Dec. 1995. Online at http://www.firstthings.com/article/2008/10/004-the-japanese-and-the-jews-24.

"In recent decades, a startlingly large number of popular books have been published in Japan": "On Ignorance, Respect and Suspicion: Current Japanese Attitudes Toward Jews," by Rotem Kowner. *Analysis of Current Trends in Antisemitism*. Vidal Sassoon International Center for the Study of Antisemitism, Hebrew University of Jerusalem, 1997. Online at http://sicsa.huji.ac.il/11kowner.htm.

CHAPTER 3. THE FACTS BEHIND THE MYTHS

Statistics about Jewish poverty in America: *Report on Jewish Poverty.* Metropolitan Council on Jewish Poverty and UJA-Federation of New York, Jan. 2004. Online at http://www.ujafedny.org/assets/documents/PDF/our-impact/caring/jewishpovertyreport.pdf.

Information about Jewish philanthropy: "Jewish Philanthropy in American Society," by Gary A. Tobin. From "Learning to Give," Web site of the League, at http://learningtogive.org/faithgroups/phil_in_america/jewish_philanthropy.asp. Also see "The History of Jewish Giving in America," by Evan Mendelson. The Jewish Virtual Library. Online at http://www.jewishvirtuallibrary.org/jsource/Judaism/philanthropy.html. Also, "The *Slate* 60: Donor Bios—The largest American charitable contributions of the year," compiled by the *Chronicle of Philanthropy,* Feb. 5, 2010. Online at http://www.slate.com/id/2243496/.

"One historian [of basketball] has commented": "The 'Scheming, Flashy Trickiness' of Basketball's Media Darlings, the Philadelphia 'Hebrews'—err . . . Sixers," by Jon Entine. *The Jewish Magazine,* July 2001. Online at http://www.jewishmag.com/45mag/basketball/basketball.htm.

"Consider this passage from a summer 2009 article about Goldman Sachs by talented journalist Matt Taibbi": "The Great American

Bubble Machine," by Matt Taibbi. *Rolling Stone,* July 9–23, 2009. On-line at http://www.rollingstone.com/politics/news/;kw=[3351,11459].

"As journalist Michael Kinsley later wrote": "How to Think About: Jewish Bankers," by Michael Kinsley. *The Atlantic Wire,* Jan. 29, 2010. Online at http://www.theatlanticwire.com/opinions/view/opinion/How-to-Think-About-Jewish-Bankers-2352.

"To cite just one example, the German economic historian Werner Sombart": Quoted in *Antisemitic Myths,* p. 85.

Quotations from Jewish teachings about the ethics of financial dealings: From *The Book of Jewish Values: A Day-by-Day Guide to Ethical Living,* by Rabbi Joseph Telushkin (New York: Bell Tower; Crown Publishing, 2000).

"In his anti-Semitic text, *On the Jews and Their Lies,* Luther wrote": Luther quotation from *On the Jews and Their Lies,* 1543; cited in *Antisemitic Myths,* pp. 45–46.

"As the scholar and wit Milton Himmelfarb famously said": "Milton Himmelfarb, Wry Essayist, Dies," by Joseph Berger. *New York Times,* Jan. 15, 2006. Online at http://query.nytimes.com/gst/fullpage.html?res=940DE3D8143FF936A25752C0A9609C8B63.

CHAPTER 4. THE STEREOTYPE TODAY

ADL attitude surveys: *American Attitudes Toward Jews in America.* Anti-Defamation League, Oct. 2009. Online at http://www.adl.org/

Anti_semitism/poll_as_2009/default.asp. *Attitudes Toward Jews in Seven European Countries.* Anti-Defamation League, Feb. 2009. Online at http://www.adl.org/Public%20ADL%20Anti-Semitism%20 Presentation%20February%202009%20_3_.pdf.

Khalil Bendib cartoon: *Cartoons and Extremism: Israel and the Jews in Arab and Western Media,* by Joel Kotek (Portland, OR: European Jewish Congress, 2008), p. 57.

"In her article 'Observations: How Suicide Bombers Are Made,' Italian journalist Fiamma Nirenstein writes": From "Observations: How Suicide Bombers Are Made," 2001; cited in *Antisemitic Myths,* p. 328.

"For example, in a 1968 conference at the University of Cairo": Quotations from *Antisemitic Myths,* pp. 317–18.

"Historian Ruth Okuneva compiled a collection of excerpts": Quotations from "Anti-Semitic Notions: Strange Analogies," 1980; cited in *Antisemitic Myths,* pp. 252–53.

"In his book *The Racist Mind,* psychologist Raphael S. Ezekiel described": Quoted in *Antisemitic Myths,* pp. 280–81.

"As I wrote in my book *Never Again?*": *Never Again? The Threat of the New Anti-Semitism,* by Abraham H. Foxman (San Francisco: Harper, 2003), pp. 31–32.

"Bayard Rustin, the famed civil rights leader and director of the A. Philip Randolph Institute": *The Anatomy of Frustration: An address delivered by Bayard Rustin, director of the A. Philip Randolph*

*Institute, at the 55th National Commission Meeting of the Anti-Defama-
tion League of B'nai B'rith.* New York: Anti-Defamation League, 1968.

"A typical passage from *The Secret Relationship*": Quoted in *Antisemitic Myths,* p. 296.

"So popular is this farrago that Henry Louis Gates": Gates quotation from "Black Demagogues and Pseudo-Scholars," 1992; cited
in *Antisemitic Myths,* p. 303.

"Historian Saul S. Friedman": Data from *Jews and the American
Slave Trade,* by Saul S. Friedman; cited in *Antisemitic Myths,* p. 294.

"A series of lectures by Farrakhan in early 2010": See "Farrakhan
in His Own Words." Anti-Defamation League, March 19, 2010. Online at http://www.adl.org/special_reports/farrakhan_own_words2/
farrakhan_own_words.asp.

"For example, in the run-up to a Tea Party protest held in San
Mateo, California": "California GOP Decries Anti-Semitic Tea Party
Activism," by Jason Linkins. *Huffington Post,* April 22, 2009. Online
at   http://www.huffingtonpost.com/2009/04/21/california-gop-de-
cries-an_n_189500.html.

"Similarly, on November 5, 2009, some five thousand activists
gathered in Washington, D.C.": "Bachmann's Capitol Tea Party: Offensive Anti-Obama Signs and Arrests." *ChattahBox,* Nov. 5, 2009.
Online at http://chattahbox.com/us/2009/11/05/bachmanns-capi-
tol-tea-party-offensive-anti-obama-signs-and-arrests/.

"For example, the ADL was alerted to an article titled 'Money Matrix'": "ADL Letter to Urban Garden Magazine." Online at http://www.adl.org/media_watch/magazines/20100122-Urban+Garden+Magazine.htm.

"In 2007, for example, former Wisconsin governor Tommy Thompson": "Republican presidential hopeful: Money-making a Jewish tradition," by Shmuel Rosner. *Haaretz*, April 29, 2007. Online at http://www.haaretz.com/hasen/spages/849062.html.

"A recent instance of ingrained stereotyping occurred in October 2009": "GOPers: DeMint Like a Jew 'Watching Our Nation's Pennies,'" by Rachel Weiner. *Huffington Post*, Oct. 19, 2009. Online at http://www.huffingtonpost.com/2009/10/19/gopers-demint-like-a-jew_n_326295.html.

"Journalist Evan Osnos recently observed": Quoted in "On China, the Economic Crisis and the Jews," by Bruce Einhorn. *BusinessWeek* "Eye on Asia." Posted Feb. 24, 2009. Online at http://www.businessweek.com/globalbiz/blog/eyeonasia/archives/2009/02/on_china_the_ec.html.

"On January 21 [2010], Limbaugh decided to address the then-current controversy": "Rush Limbaugh Tries to Enlist 'Jewish Bankers' Against Obama," by David Gibson. *Politics Daily*, Jan. 22, 2010. Online at http://www.politicsdaily.com/2010/01/22/rush-limbaugh-tries-to-enlist-jewish-bankers-against-obama/.

"In commenting on this in his *Forward* column, J. J. Goldberg. . .": "Foxman Fever Doesn't Discriminate," by J. J. Goldberg, *The Forward*, Feb. 10, 2010. Online at http://www.forward.com/article/125423/.

Ilan Halimi case: "Paris: Gang suspected of killing Jew nabbed," by Hannah Senesh. *Ynet News* (Israel), Feb. 19, 2006. Online at http://www.freerepublic.com/focus/news/1581534/posts. "Tale of torture and murder horrifies whole of France," by Michel Gurfinkiel. *New York Sun,* Feb. 22, 2006. Online at http://www.nysun.com/foreign/tale-of-torture-and-murder-horrifies-the-whole/27948/.

CHAPTER 5. WHEN EVERYONE
HAS A MEGAPHONE

Haiti "organ harvesting" story: "How One Man's Rant Spread Globally," by Abraham H. Foxman. *Cutting Edge News,* Jan. 25, 2010. Online at http://www.adl.org/ADL_Opinions/Israel/CuttingEdgeNews_012510.htm.

Anti-Semitic online responses to financial crisis of 2008–2009: "Blaming the Jews: Reaction to the Financial Crisis in Europe, Latin America and the Middle East." Anti-Defamation League, Oct. 31, 2008. Online at http://www.adl.org/main_Anti_Semitism_International/Financial_Crisis.

"Researchers at the Digital Hate and Terrorism project of the Simon Wiesenthal Center (SWC)": *Facebook, YouTube +: How Social*

Media Outlets Impact Digital Terrorism and Hate. Simon Wiesenthal Center, 2009. Online at http://www.wiesenthal.com/atf/cf/%7B54d3 85e6-f1b9-4e9f-8e94-890c3e6dd277%7D/NY-RELEASE.PDF.

CHAPTER 6. NOT SO FUNNY

"I am holding in my hand a book": *Jewtopia: The Chosen Book for the Chosen People* by Bryan Fogel and Sam Wolfson (New York: Warner Books, 2006).

"Hence the culture of what writer Marnie Winston-Macauley refers to": "Are Jewish Stereotypes Funny? Part 3," by Marnie Winston-Macauley. *Aish.* Online at http://www.aish.com/j/fs/48965451.html.

Details about *Borat:* "Not Very Nice—The Borat movie: They botched the joke," by Ron Rosenbaum. *Slate,* Nov. 2, 2006. Online at http://www.slate.com/id/2152772.

"The most biting critique": "*The Passion of the Christ* Fuels Antisemitism—On *South Park,*" by Max Gross. *Jewish Daily Forward,* April 9, 2004. Online at http://www.forward.com/articles/5445/.

CHAPTER 7. DAMNED IF WE DO, DAMNED IF WE DON'T

"In other cases, it can be much more disabling, as eloquently described in a newspaper column": "Jews Without Money" by Yonnasan

Gershom. Minneapolis: *The Alley,* 1986. Online at http://www.pine net.com/~rooster/poorjews.html.

"The somewhat perverse emotional effects on Jews of this kind of hostile environment": "Are Jews Smarter?" by Jennifer Senior. *New York,* Oct. 16, 2005. Online at http://nymag.com/nymetro/news/culture/features/1478/.

"No less a cultural icon than America's greatest humorist, Mark Twain": *Concerning the Jews,* by Mark Twain. *Harper's New Monthly Magazine,* March 1898. Reprinted New York: Anti-Defamation League, 2002.

"In her book *In Cheap We Trust: The Story of a Misunderstood American Virtue,* journalist Lauren Weber": *In Cheap We Trust,* p. 128.

"In his recent book *Capitalism and the Jews,* historian Jerry Z. Muller": *Capitalism and the Jews,* p. 129.

"If you wonder whether tensions between Christians and Jews": "Jews and Money: When Anti-Semitism Isn't," by Rabbi Avi Shafran. *Jewish World Review,* no date. Online at http://www.jewishworld review.com/avi/shafran_money.php3.

"In his marvelous *Book of Jewish Values: A Day-by-Day Guide to Ethical Living,* Rabbi Joseph Telushkin": p. 96.

INDEX